EVENTUALLY

D1643028

30130 137632278

EVENTUALLY

Concluding the memories of
"Adamant Eve"

1955 – 1995

Eve Day

ISIS

LARGE PRINT
Oxford

Copyright © Eve Day, 2003

First published in Great Britain 2004
by
Isis Publishing Ltd

Published in Large Print 2004 by ISIS Publishing Ltd,
7 Centremead, Osney Mead, Oxford OX2 0ES
by arrangement with the author

The author can be contacted at
evelday@bigpond.com

All rights reserved

The moral right of the author has been asserted

British Library Cataloguing in Publication Data
Day, Eve,
    Eventually : concluding the memories of
    "Adamant Eve". – Large print ed. –
    (Reminiscence)
    1. Day, Eve
    2. Large type books
    3. Great Britain – Social conditions – 1945–
    4. Great Britain – Biography
    I. Title
    941.085'092

ISBN 0–7531–9952–1 (hb)
ISBN 0–7531–9953–X (pb)

Printed and bound by Antony Rowe, Chippenham

ESSEX COUNTY COUNCIL
LIBRARIES

Dedicated to the memory of Oliver
and for all my dear grandchildren
Katie, Rachel, Max, Sarah, John,
Simon and Rowan

Acknowledgments

I am indebted
To Kath Keating for her discernment and support,
To Anne Walsh for her assurance and approval and
To Erica Gamble who patiently typed the manuscript.

A sense of humour is as important to life
as shock absorbers are to car,

It helps us over the bumps . . .

I can think of nothing apter
Than a verse to start each chapter.

Contents

PART ONE

PART TWO

Foreword

In this third volume of Eve's trilogy we travel with her from her wedding day to the day of her retirement. This journey takes us from England to literally the other end of the earth — Perth, Western Australia with all the fears and surprises such a lifestyle change must involve.

Among the qualities that travel with Eve and transplant very well are her enthusiasm for new experiences, her joyous sense of humour and her great loyalty to friends on either side of the globe. Happy reading.

Kath Keating.

Foreword

Hans Küng

PART ONE

CHAPTER ONE

The Honeymoon is Over

In one small room we managed to cook and eat and sleep. Appendicitis suddenly. Spilt oxtail made me weep.

After our wedding in Guildford, Surrey, one chilly March afternoon in 1955, Don and I spent a few days in Ventnor on the Isle of Wight. I had worn a borrowed wedding dress and Mrs Cooper, a good friend, had made the bouquets and wedding cake, a very generous gift. I paid for the reception myself. The bill of fourteen pounds nine shillings and ten pence left us with very little cash. Fortunately, many of my relatives had given money as gifts (maybe a Jewish tradition?) which we saved for an emergency.

In 1955 accommodation was a major problem. Don's Aunt Glad and Uncle Arthur kindly rented us the front bedroom of their small semi-detached house in Chingford on the outskirts of North London. The twelve by ten foot room contained our double bed, table and chairs and a tiny electric "Baby Belling" cooking stove. Everything we owned we stored in the wardrobe and a pile of suitcases. Amazingly we lived in these extremely restricted quarters for two and a half years.

Don's main employment was as a technician in the Mechanical Engineering Department of King's College in The Strand. To enable us to acquire a home of our own, he took a second job. This consisted of teaching evening classes at Hackney Technical College in Workshop Technology and other allied subjects. Each day he travelled to central London, usually on his motor bike. This almost silent vehicle, an L.E. Velocette, was also the model used by the police. On evening class days he bought himself a light meal at one of the local cafés, always fish and chips or poached eggs on toast. He was convinced they were safe to eat in this rather doubtful area. Uncle Harry once quoted, "What will you have?" asked the waiter, quietly picking his nose.

"I'll have two hard boiled eggs, you rotter, you can't stick your finger in those."

I returned to our room after working all day as a Comptometer Operator and invariably made myself baked beans on toast. On the evenings Don taught, I cycled laboriously up the hill to Chingford Hospital, where I was employed as a part-time auxiliary nurse from six until nine o'clock, covering the time when the day and night staff exchanged duties. My few years nursing training in Guildford had not been totally wasted. Once again I found myself chanting the nightly invitation to the patients "Tea, coffee, cocoa, Ovaltine or Bovril?" reminding me of my days at St Luke's Hospital.

During the time I nursed there, Don's younger sister Gwenda developed tuberculosis and was admitted to Chingford Hospital. Always very petite and looking rather frail, her now pallid face accentuated her fragility. I felt upset to see her in this weak, debilitated state. Fortunately the symptoms had been diagnosed early and she eventually made a full recovery. Fresh air being considered essential to the cure of this insidious disease, patients were nursed in individual chalets with one side open to the elements. I was able to combine my nursing duties with a quick visit to my new sister-in-law.

Don's elder sister Win, who had tried hard to "match make" for us, was frustrated to be in Sierra Leone at the time our wedding. Will, her husband had been transferred there with his Regiment. Soon after we married, she returned to England alone for a few months and stayed with a friend, pregnant with her third child. Each birth had needed to be by caesarean section as, like Gwenda, she was very small. Andrew arrived when Stephen was seven and Valerie fourteen.

One evening, after we had been married about six months, Don was downstairs playing his ritual weekly game of Cribbage with his Uncle Arthur. They continued this until we moved some years later. Engrossed in completing the ironing in our cramped room upstairs, I doubled over with a severe abdominal pain. "Oh dear, I had better lie down" I thought, but the pain persisted. Dare I go and tell Don? No, grin and bear it. After I had vomited a couple of times and was feeling very unwell, I fearfully tiptoed downstairs and hesitantly intruded on their game. Don was not pleased to be interrupted but realised I was in severe pain and sent for the doctor. When he arrived, he felt all over my abdomen and when he pressed my right side I realised the origin of the pain. To my surprise he announced, "Appendicitis, straight to hospital."

They admitted me to Whipps Cross Hospital in Walthamstow immediately and operated the following morning. Fortunately the straightforward procedure had no complications and they discharged me after five days. Convalescing at home for a further week was recommended.

A day that stays vividly in my mind was attempting to cook oxtail soup in my new pressure cooker. I meticulously followed the recipe on my first ambitious venture. Unaware of the necessity to release the valve at the correct time, the lid blew off with an almighty blast.

Splash, splatter, splosh, greasy dark brown gravy gushed glutinously everywhere. It dripped all over the stove, trickled down the wall and streamed in an oily cascade over the edge of the pan.

"Oh, what shall I do, what shall I do?" In tears I gasped at the mess and didn't know where to start cleaning it up. I knew Don would be severely displeased, worrying about the damage to his Uncle's room. I cleaned up the best I could, still weeping and just felt as if I wanted to go home to Mum! Alas, I had no home other than this small room and my mother was long since dead. I knew no one in the area, how could I escape to regain my equilibrium? My refuge in all times of stress was the library. Fortunately it was still open. I sheltered in its comforting anonymity until I felt strong enough to return and face the remnants of the offensive mess. Ugh!

CHAPTER
TWO

Motorbike
and Minicar

Operas and holidays. With Cornwall I was charmed.
Accident in minicar. No one badly harmed.

Occasionally at weekends we went coarse fishing on the River Lea or to Broxbourne in Hertfordshire. I learned some of the techniques of casting, also how to sit still and keep quiet. We caught nothing edible although, to my delight, I did once land a reasonably sized tench.

Our room was no place for relaxation, so we went out most weekends. Sometimes we just went out for a ride into the countryside. Occasionally we drove to Surrey to visit Dad or see Diddley or some of my friends in Guildford. Often a sunny day would see us heading for the South Coast.

Whilst I was at work sometimes Don phoned me, "I've got tickets for Covent Garden to see 'Tosca' " or maybe, "I've managed to get a couple of gallery seats at Sadlers Wells" — or, "We'll go and see 'The Gondoliers' at the Savoy, meet you at the usual place and time."

8

King's College being situated in central London, Don was often able to buy cancelled tickets for that evening. I would catch the number thirty-eight bus from Chingford and meet Don outside the "Quality Inn" restaurant in Leicester Square. This American owned establishment had an elaborately descriptive menu, such as "Aunt Mary's home baked deep filled apple pie".

"I'd love one of their famous three decker sandwiches," I'd say.

These had various fillings named for different U.S. states like the "Kentucky" or the "Colorado". Afterwards, ignoring the temptation of the well-advertised apple pie, I enjoyed a waffle with maple syrup. Then we walked to the theatre, enjoyed the show and returned home either by bus or on the motor bike.

Once we went to The Royal Theatre, Edmonton, to see the Carl Rosa Opera perform "Il Trovatore". The actors, like most of the audience, relied on public transport to take them home. The opera was running a bit late and I will never forget their rendering of Leonora's aria at double speed — it would have made an excellent comedy item.

The year after we married, we had a very enjoyable holiday at Fowey in Cornwall. We boarded with George and Alice who lived at the top of the exceptionally steep street. Later we referred to them as "the robbers of Fowey" as their catering was extremely frugal. They exuded malapropisms. Don and I found it hard to keep a straight face when Alice referred to George drinking his beer from a "tanker" and she wouldn't be long, she was just going to put some "massacre" on her eyelashes. They awoke at the "crank" of dawn.

Another year we stayed at a farm in Kingsteignton, a small charming village in South Devon between Teignmouth and Newton Abbott. I really enjoyed the farm atmosphere as well as the plentiful well-cooked food. Peter, the farmer's son, discovered my fascination for pigs and delighted in showing me the latest litter. I would have been perfectly happy just mooching around the farm, but we wanted to take advantage of the good weather and explore some of the quaint and charming villages that abounded in Devon, and also the moors.

One outing saw us passing through Barnstaple —

"Oh please can we stop" I begged Don. "It says 'Annual Fair'. I'd love to see it."

We parked the motor bike and enjoyed the colourful festivities. We tried the traditional coconut shy. Don having a steady hand, won one — I won a soft toy at a skittle game, but our triumph of the day was Don's watch. There were a number of machines where one put in a coin and *tried* to guide a crane to pick up various tempting items embedded in coloured stones. A really good prize such as a watch was a magnet for the gullible public. I have mentioned that Don had a steady hand. On his second attempt, with great skill, he guided the crane to grip the watch and drop it down the chute. We were triumphant. The owner was mortified that his "treasure" had been won and we left him frustratingly trying the crane himself.

Don decided that the motor bike was a bit uncomfortable for us in the uncertain climate of

Britain. In the mid-fifties a few types of small three-wheeler cars could be seen on the roads, the Heinkel, the Reliant and the Bond minicar. All of these could be driven using a motor cycle licence as they had no reverse. We decided on a Bond minicar with a 197 cc motor bike engine, very economical.

One day we were on our way to the Laundrette on Chingford High Road, a very busy major road in North London. Our dirty clothes were piled behind my seat in a large bag. Suddenly Don realised he was unable to steer the vehicle at all. We discovered later that the pin in the steering wheel had become dislodged. Fortunately we veered to the left where the little car wrapped itself around a concrete lamp post. A passer-by took a photo of the dramatic scene that was printed on the front page of the local newspaper the following week with the headline, "Two Escaped In This Crash."

We were incredibly lucky. Had the car veered to the right we could have collided with a big, red, double decker bus.

An ambulance arrived quite quickly. We were both pretty shaken, no seat belts in those days. Directly we arrived at Whipps Cross Hospital (where I had recently been a patient with my appendectomy), we were rushed to Casualty.

Don spat out glass fragments from his mouth. His face was covered in superficial scratches but no broken bones. His permanent dimple in one cheek is a legacy from that accident. I broke two ribs, very painful. In those days they strapped them tightly, I also had quite a few bruises. We were extremely lucky to have suffered

11

nothing worse and we were insured, but of course now without a vehicle. Whatever happened to our washing that day?

CHAPTER
THREE

When I Was a Spy

At Lebus's I had a job and learned to be a spy.
The Agency had varied work where I'd diversify.

When I moved to Chingford, I had no problem getting employment. There were a lot of advertisements in the local paper for qualified comptometer operators. The efficient training I received at the Ministry of Food proved to be a blessing during the first few years of married life. I was definitely working for *money*, not for love of the job. This qualification was far better paid than if I'd sought employment in child care. We were determined to save to buy our own home, particularly as neither of us had had a proper home for so very many years. A well paid job was vital.

After some deliberation, I applied and was accepted to work as a "comp" operator in the Sales Research Department of Harris Lebus. The two sons of the original "Harris", Oliver and Anthony, ran the firm. At that time, in the fifties, we were told it was the largest furniture factory in the world. Situated in Tottenham, North East London, it involved two short bus rides from Chingford. The furniture they produced, a

13

medium quality, hard wearing product, was sold mainly to the many commercial hotels that abounded in England in those days. Often, when watching the re-run of an old film, I spot a Lebus wardrobe or toilet. The word "toilet" of course, was the correct name for a dressing table. I have always found it strange to use the word for a lavatory.

We were a happy group. Mr Bridges and Mr Lenton were in charge of the department. Reg Smythe, the typist Vera's husband, had just started selling the books of his cartoons. Still in its infancy then, the Andy Capp series has remained immensely popular. Mary, Betty and Joyce were my colleagues. Joyce and Tom Uff were childless, but said if they ever produced a son they would name him Justin! Our work consisted mainly of calculating statistics and forecasting sales. One memorable day we had an official visit from His Royal Highness the Duke of Edinburgh. All the office staff lined up to greet him as he entered the factory. He walked along in traditional style with his hands clasped behind him, acknowledging us by smiling to each side as he was escorted by Oliver, Anthony and the other important personages.

One day I received a summons from Mr Bridges.

"The Furniture Show and the Ideal Homes Exhibition will be on in a few weeks time, would you be happy to find out certain facts for us if we gave you and your husband complimentary tickets?"

"Yes, certainly, we were hoping to go if we could have afforded it."

I studied the list of tasks. I had to discover if a certain firm was about to produce a high-backed dining chair, and similar detailed facts from various rivals. Don and I, being a newly married couple, were naturally interested in furniture and no one would have suspected us of "snooping". After I had asked each pertinent question and received the necessary information, I made a dash for the "Ladies" to enable me to record it in my notebook. I was then able to report the relevant details to Mr Bridges the following day.

The Show in the enormous Stadium at Earls Court we found bewildering, with the quantity of firms showing furniture.

"Oh look Don, I like that dark traditional style over there."

We admired the attractive, very expensive items by Ercolani, using their trade name Ercol. This furniture has remained popular but the prices of their solid wood furniture is now prohibitive. We did eventually buy their lounge chairs covered in Sanderson's linen with a delightful Jacobean design in autumn colours. Their dining suite and sideboard we still have, solid wood furniture rarely deteriorates.

Occasionally, when we were extra busy or staff were sick or on holidays, girls from a local agency came as relief. I became very friendly with June who told me of the generous rates of pay and decided it was time for a change.

I joined the Essex Calculating Service and remained with them for some years, even after we eventually moved. I travelled everywhere by public transport and

15

was given an allowance according to distance. In those days the mail was very reliable, two deliveries each day. Each Friday I received a letter with my instructions for the following week.

Don often laughed in later days, saying, "You name a firm or factory in or around London and Eve has worked there."

The variety was extensive and I rarely stayed with one business longer than a few weeks. Occasionally I was requested to return when they needed relief staff again. The famous company of Reeves Artists Supplies in Enfield needed me at stocktaking time, as did "Aquascutum" of Regent Street. I had to learn special methods to calculate the area of timber when I worked for a large importers in Bethnal Green. In Leadenhall Street in the City, I helped to calculate various interesting insurance claims. Here we were given Luncheon Vouchers that enabled us to have a meal at a variety of restaurants sporting the pertinent logo. Nearby Walthamstow housed a large office of the London Electricity Board. Here I became part of a large "comp" pool doing wages.

My favourite venue, Brooke Bond's, the famous tea firm, saw me doing wages amongst other things. The tea sorters received a bonus of sixpence for each beetle they found. Some received an extra seven or eight shillings a week in their pay packets. Was that really tea that we bought or just beetles' legs? No humble canteen there as in many firms, but an excellent subsidised restaurant. All the office staff ate there, from the top management to the humble clerk. Initially I worked at their original buildings just off Petticoat Lane. A year or two later, when Miss Parkes asked for me again, the brand new building was in the shadow of St Paul's Cathedral. Many new offices were being constructed in that area which had received severe bombing during the war. It was a miracle that St Paul's survived. Another reason I loved working at Brooke Bond's was that we were allowed to buy one pound of tea a week at half price. It was there that I started trying various teas, and Don became quite a connoisseur.

That was another inducement working for so many different businesses. We could very often buy goods at a discount price. I bought paints at Reeves, and brassières from Exquisite Form Brassières in Edmonton. The bras had circles of stitches that formed a rather unnerving cone, the fashion of the time. The work there was varied and interesting — wages and statistics.

The large department store in the West End, Bourne and Hollingsworth, needed relief staff for a week. I felt most conspicuous wearing a floral summer dress when the rest of the office staff were soberly clad in black. The supervisor, a real tartar, even timed us in the lavatory. I was petrified of her and relieved to be sent elsewhere the following week.

Each December all the local Woolworths employed us agency girls to do the annual stocktaking. After Christmas, we went en masse to their main office in my favourite part of London, Oxford Street. Here we worked at pressure, boring but not difficult, adding interminable columns of figures, checking all the local shops' results. My Christmas present from Don was money to spend at the Sales, so for a couple of years I was in the right place at the right time, as Woolworths was situated in the hub of the West End.

The comptometer resembled a large typewriter and was the main method for calculations long before the invention of the electronic calculator. It performed a wide variety of functions, even square roots when necessary. It took a fair bit of skill to operate, hence our good salary of about eighteen pounds a month, excellent money in those days. Everything needed to be converted to decimals. I remember a ha'penny was .00283 recurring as a decimal of a pound — what useless knowledge now. We had a variety of conversion charts as all measurements, weights and areas were Imperial.

Each Friday it was exciting to read my letter to discover my next destination. Occasionally it was greeted with a groan, but I was most fortunate having such a variety of interesting and stimulating jobs as well as the occasional mundane one. I continued working for the agency after we moved until the next big event in my life. Although I had always hated the idea of office work, with this variety, how could I be bored?

CHAPTER
FOUR

"Wildthorne"

Moving from our modest room to a bungalow.
Buying lovely china and a kettle just for show.

The tiny room in which we cooked, ate and slept was only meant to be temporary, although we actually survived in that claustrophobic environment for two and a half years. We saved very hard, both of us working at two jobs.

Some of the small towns in Essex were expanding and this interested us as we did not want to remain in London. Those not too close to Outer London had reasonably priced plots of land. We found a builder who had contracted to build a small group of two-bedroom semi-detached bungalows in a town called Wickford. This was situated about thirty miles east of London on the Southend rail line, with easy access to the City.

The cost including the land was £1650. Ours was £1750 as we bought the corner plot with extra land, nearly a quarter of an acre. Often at weekends we visited Wickford on our motor bike, and later the mini-car. We watched the progress being made on the foundations of the eight semi-detached bungalows and the detached one, our neighbour. We were situated on a triple intersection of Swan Lane, Brock Hill, and we were the last house in Church End Lane. This area is called Runwell, after the ancient church of "Our Lady of the Running Well" still in use.

Houses had no numbers, but each was named. Some like "Dunroamin" or "Journey's End" were very common. Some were named after a favourite holiday town "Polperro" or "Windermere".

"What shall we name our house?" I asked Don. "I know, what about 'Wildthorne', with our dense hedge of hawthorn, honeysuckle, wild roses and brambles?"

Don agreed and we had an attractive sign made for the gate. Later we received numbers, ours was 125. Until then, visitors who came by rail and asked a local person directions to Church End Lane, were sent a mile along Runwell Road, then up the long hill of Church End Lane, two sides of a triangle, scrutinising the name on every house each side of the road. If we were expecting them, we gave them directions to come up Swan Lane and our house was at the intersection. The area was known as the Wantz or Wantz Corner. This is an old Essex word for "Crossroads". It was very useful to have a bus stop, letter box and phone box outside our gate. We had no telephone in the house during our nine years there, and no car.

Each visit we made, we visualised where each room would be, the sitting/dining room, small kitchen, bathroom and two bedrooms. It was most disconcerting to see no progress being made. We tried to 'phone the builder to no avail.

Eventually we received a letter to say that he had gone into receivership and we were to attend a solicitor's office in London. Nine couples arrived, each eyeing the others with interest. Most of us were young, but a few were older, buying these small bungalows to achieve their ambition to retire in the country. The solicitor explained that a new builder would be found and that other than an annoying delay, we would not be penalised financially, a great relief to us all.

Our regular Sunday afternoon visits continued until at last, in the summer of 1957, the exciting day arrived when we were able to move in. We had no regrets saying goodbye to the small room. We owned few possessions although I did have an iron and ironing board from my single days and a few other necessities.

Houses did not include appliances such as gas stoves, floorcoverings, curtains or light fittings. We haunted the shops trying to make decisions. Initially we paid extra to have good quality Marley vinyl floor tiles fitted throughout, so only needed a couple of rugs. A fridge was not an essential and normally would have been something we might have bought later. We decided to use the money we received from the insurance company for the wrecked minicar to buy one. We chose Frigidaire, as we knew the reliability of this firm. Aunt Bess possessed a "monster" one in her large home in Eastbourne which was quite ancient and still functioning. The copper to boil the washing resided under the draining board in the kitchen.

We had ample opportunity to decide on furniture whilst I had been employed at Lebus's and visited many exhibitions. It was exciting choosing our Ercol designs. We favoured the traditional look of the deep comfortable arm chairs and decided on the new high-backed Windsor dining chairs in dark elm and beechwood.

Out of necessity, I needed to develop domestic accomplishments fast. At my various schools during my fragmented childhood I had never had the opportunity to learn Domestic Science. At boarding school we darned socks, sewed on buttons and did embroidery. Curtains needed to be made, so I bought a second hand, rather ancient, Wheeler and Wilson hand sewing machine. I tried to master its intricacies and moods. It sounds amazing nowadays, but until I met Don, I had never heard anyone swear. I knew the words existed but actually hearing someone using them, was totally alien to my rather genteel if varied upbringing. The very first time the word "bloody" emitted from *my* lips was with that unco-operative sewing machine. No instructions came with it so that it was by trial and error and a lot of persistence that I finally made all the curtains for the house.

I felt so happy to have the security of a real home at last, probably the first I could call "mine" since I was a very small child.

Once we were settled in, I withdrew our wedding present money that had been residing in my Post Office Savings Bank. I separated the amounts meticulously that had been given as gifts from various relatives. Now I could indulge in spending it on both necessities and inclinations. I had always yearned for Wedgwood willow pattern china. One aunt's contribution bought the dinner service for six, complete with tureens; another aunt, the tea set, and yet another aunt, the breakfast set. This included egg cups and very large cups and saucers. Sadly I rarely used this china as it was extraordinarily brittle and cracked or chipped so very easily — a real liability.

Some years later we bought some attractive melamine ware for everyday family use. I have always loved elegant china and slowly, oh so slowly, I built up a comprehensive set of attractive Royal Doulton translucent china. This service, in the design "Pillar Rose", as well as being very delicate looking, unlike the willow pattern, is extremely robust. A few years ago, sadly I dropped two dinner plates on to the tiled kitchen floor. They shattered dramatically into tiny smithereens but none of it has ever chipped or cracked. I bought it piece by piece, saving a little money each week from my housekeeping allowance.

Now in our own home, I could "play houses" to my heart's content. I took great pride in polishing our new furniture and keeping the place meticulous. A few silver items had been given to us as gifts apart from the dressing table set I had inherited, and I slowly collected some attractive brass and copper ware. They looked perfect displayed around our rustic brick fireplace. During one of our outings to Plymouth in Devon, we saw a *real* copper kettle in an antique shop, one that had actually been used over a fire. The base took an enormous amount of elbow grease and Brasso to get it clean. It dates back to 1790 and we got it for a reasonable price as one brass acorn fitting on the side of the wooden handle was missing. Don cleverly made a replacement. Each week I enjoyed cleaning my increasing collection of silver, copper and brass. I have always found it a very satisfactory occupation ever since my weekly task of cleaning all Mrs Dixon's brass door knobs when I was ten.

My trusty bicycle, shared by the two of us, was the only vehicle we now possessed. We walked to and from the station each day to travel to Liverpool Street Station in London. Occasionally my work would take me to Romford, Ilford, Stratford or other destinations on the line. Then it invariably meant a long walk or a bus ride, so I needed to leave home very early each day. I often took the short cut across the field but only when the weather was dry. Returning home it did not matter if my shoes were caked with mud on the frequent rainy days. During the winter, it was dark when I left home and also when I returned.

In 1958 Don changed from being a technician at King's College and teaching evening classes at Hackney Tech to becoming a full time teacher there, in Workshop Technology. This involved him catching another train from Liverpool Street to Hackney. Fortunately the College was adjacent to the station. After a few years, as well as daytime teaching, he taught three evenings too. This entitled him to one day off a week, so he only worked there three long days and one with normal hours.

Now that we were in our own home we did not go out at weekends, both for practical and financial reasons.

One day when Win and Will, recently returned from Africa, visited us, Will said, "We were not able to be with you at your wedding and we would like to take you out. Would you like to come to a matinée with us?"

What a memorable Saturday that was. Will had managed with great difficulty, to get tickets for "My Fair Lady", the musical adaptation of George Bernard Shaw's "Pygmalion". At the time it was the most popular show in the West End. Rex Harrison featured as Professor Higgins, Stanley Holloway was outrageous as Eliza Doolittle's father and the new, young actress Julie Andrews starred in the title role.

We went to an Indian Restaurant after the show for a delicious meal, a real treat. I expect their daughter Valerie would have been old enough to baby-sit Stephen and little Andrew who was a toddler. We were childless then, so had no such problems.

Everyone hummed the songs from the show. My favourite was

> All I want is a place somewhere,
> Far away from the cold night air,
> And one enormous chair
> Ow, wouldn't it be loverley.

Some years later, Marion aged three, who also loved the song, innocently asked, "Mummy, sing me the wooden tit song."

CHAPTER
FIVE

Washing Day

Boil clothes in the copper, rinse them in the sink. Soak and scrub and washboard, hoping they don't shrink.

Washing was a problem when we were first married, (not ourselves, our clothes) and involved much more planning and time than the small amount of laundry warranted.

Each Tuesday the laundry was sent and delivered. Sheets and towels returned pressed and spotless as did Don's white collars and shirts that needed stiff starching. These were the days when collar studs were used, as were cuff-links.

I sighed.

"Oh dear, how am I going to wash our 'smalls'?"

"What about the bathroom handbasin?" Don answered sensibly.

So that is what I did, instead of using the bowl rigged up on a board over the bath that we used for washing our dishes.

I always felt a trespasser, walking through Aunt Glad's kitchen to hang things on the washing line. This ran adjacent to a path the length of the garden. I negotiated a suitable time so I would not monopolise the line when she needed it. Saturday fortunately suited her as, with both of us working, that was our main washing day. We packed the dirty articles into a large linen bag, the same one I had used at boarding school, and off we went on the motor bike or later the minicar, to the local laundrette.

When we moved to the bungalow in Wickford, we became proud possessors of a gas copper to boil the clothes in. Anything really soiled needed soaking first. I then used the glass washboard over the sink to scrub them. Lux soap flakes were used. I patiently stood and rotated the hand agitator as the clothes revolved in the steaming water. Big wooden tongs were used to lift out the garments into our large, glazed, earthenware sink for rinsing. The white articles were rinsed a second time in water tinted a delicate blue. I had swished the blue bag into it first. This little bag containing a solid blue block lasted many washes. Then came the tricky bit — starching. Powdered starch was mixed to a smooth paste with cold water, then boiling water was added slowly as I briskly stirred the mixture. A clear gel formed that I poured into a bowl and diluted in hot water. I then immersed Don's collars, shirt cuffs, tablecloths and anything else that needed starching.

Back to the copper again. It had the latest luxury, a folding rubber wringer that extracted most of the water from the washing. The scullery of the older homes still often housed a mangle with wooden rollers. This small room adjoined the kitchen and had a door into the garden. It contained a large sink used for flower arrangements and the weekly wash. When one came in muddy from outside, the Wellington boots were removed and kept there on a rack.

Modern homes like ours had no scullery so the copper fitted under the draining board. One day I pulled it out to use it and to my horror found a snake coiled up underneath. I quickly slapped the dustbin lid over it. A short while later the gas man came to read the meter.

"Could you do a little job for me?"

"Sure, missus," he answered confidently. He blanched when I said, "There is a snake under that lid, could you please remove it so that I can replace the copper?"

He used the long tongs and eventually plucked up the courage to flip it outside to our mutual relief.

The fields and hedgerows around us probably had many such reptiles. The harmless grass snake must have slithered in unnoticed. I *did* see an adder up Brock Hill some years later when I was bluebelling with the children in what we called "Goldilocks Wood". The adder, or viper as it is also called, is England's only poisonous snake.

> Why did the viper vipe 'er nose?
> Because the adder 'ad 'er 'ankerchief!

Drying the washing was always a problem in such an uncertain climate. On many days it rained or snowed or just drizzled. Sometimes I was fortunate enough to dry it outside, pegged to the washing line. Gypsies occasionally knocked on the door selling pegs made from chestnut wood. I had a mixture of these and the wooden spring pegs. A tall forked prop lifted the line high to flap enthusiastically in the wind. My small spin dryer was a boon. This and the copper both had taps at the base that needed emptying into a bucket. In the winter I spread the nappies over the radiator and hung clothes on an airer in front of the fire. Alas, this made the garments hard and rough; nothing compares with sunshine and a nice breeze to dry the washing.

The only item we ever bought on hire purchase was, when my youngest child was two and I had a part time job, the latest thing — a Hoover twin tub washing machine. Luxury at last.

CHAPTER SIX

Flooded Home and Arrival of Marion

The flood was really frightening, still we both survived.
Rushed off in the ambulance, then Marion arrived.

The day arrived when I realised I was pregnant. My first sign was not fancying a cup of tea, most unlike me. In subsequent pregnancies, I realised immediately what that aversion indicated. I did tell Don, but superstitiously kept it a secret until I was past the twelve week "danger period" for miscarriages. I could have kept it a secret throughout the pregnancy as to my disappointment I hardly showed at all, maybe due to my wide hips. In those days one wore a smock, almost as a badge of achievement. I bought a very smart turquoise linen smock and adjustable skirt set and hardly wore it.

Unfortunately not only did I suffer from morning sickness, but that and constant nausea continued for the long nine months. No wonder that at term I weighed the same as before the pregnancy.

I continued working until six weeks before the baby was due, to enable me to qualify for the lump sum payment from the National Health Insurance. After marriage, one could opt to pay only sixpence a week as a working woman. Benefits were available to women who continued paying the weekly four and sixpence as a single woman. Oh, how glad I am *now* that I paid the full amount, as it entitles me to qualify for a part U.K. pension. I worked out that I had been employed for nine years and ten months. They must have given me the benefit of the doubt for the minimum qualification is ten years. Each morning I caught the train to London that started from Wickford. Two other passengers, Colin and Bob always kindly saved the window seat for me. Bob had a young family, Colin was a bachelor who loved children. I really appreciated their concern and interest.

During my last few weeks, I attended the pre-natal classes held at the Clinic. There I met a lot of ladies, some of them sporting very large bumps and many only six months pregnant. We learned breathing exercises, information on what to expect during labour and finished with relaxation classes, when I invariably fell asleep.

September 1958 saw some of the worst floods the south east of England had endured for many years. Nearby Canvey Island was completely under water and a double decker bus was stranded in Wickford High Street.

Our home was situated half way up a long hill. The water rushed down in such a deluge that many houses including our bungalow were flooded. Wise neighbours had raised their bed and other pieces of furniture on towers of tinned food, very inventive. How glad I was then, just a few weeks before my baby was due, to be still reasonably agile. We watched apprehensively as the murky water started seeping under the doors. It was useless to try and sweep it out, although we did initially attempt to. We had no second storey to retreat to which was very frightening at the time. We lifted everything we could off the floor, and paddled around anxiously hoping the rain would stop and the floods subside. It did eventually, to our great relief. The water had reached about eighteen inches throughout the house leaving a tidemark and a filthy, muddy residue. Afterwards Don made flood boards that were fixed to all the external doors with plasticine to seal them. One needed to step over the two feet high barricade to enter or exit the house, but later they also acted as an efficient childproof barrier.

We had one big problem during this crisis —

"Oh dear, Timmy needs to go out and dig a hole, whatever shall we do?"

Timmy, who turned out to be a female, was our cherished tabby cat. How would she cope in such a predicament? Fortunately, Don had a heap of soil where he had been digging. Now it was mud, but at least some of it emerged from the water. He tenderly carried her out and back again after she had "performed". She then settled in a comfortable armchair after cleaning herself so that she was able to supervise the tedious cleaning up procedure. Thank God we were covered by insurance as some items needed replacing. I'm sure it did no good to the stove or fridge. We were luckier than some, who lost so many of their possessions.

The following month, I celebrated my twenty-eighth birthday and the next evening went into labour about a week earlier than expected. An ambulance took me to St Andrews Hospital, Billericay, about four miles away. How glad we were to have the telephone box outside our door. Early the following morning, at eight o'clock just when the day staff were relieving the night staff, after eight hours labour I produced a little girl. Immediately after birth, she looked startlingly like Don, but this similarity diminished later. I was so thrilled with her. The tiny, perfect hands and feet fascinated me. We had discussed names for months and agreed that with, such a short surname, two- three-syllable names would make the recitation of them sound more musical. We also did not want one that would be abbreviated. We both liked "Marion" and gave her "Winifred" as a second name after Don's sister. We took great care that her initials would be innocuous. All Don's life he has endured D.A.D. chosen for him by his sister Win.

The second day, instead of awakening to see her crib by my bed, it had gone.

"Where is my baby?" I asked frantically.

"She is in the nursery, there are just a few complications, nothing to worry about," the officious Sister informed me briskly.

I felt bewildered and very frightened in the large hospital ward. The other mothers were nursing their babies and I was desperately worried. In those days they never explained conditions to patients.

Eventually I discovered her severe jaundice was due to "Haemorrhagic disease of the newborn" which is not very uncommon. The poor little baby's tiny heels were a mass of bruises from the frequent blood tests.

She was stabilised in a few days and all went well. After the usual two weeks hospitalisation, we were discharged. Don collected us in a taxi.

Another phase of my life began; a beginning that would never end — motherhood.

CHAPTER
SEVEN

Babies

Pregnancies, deliveries of babies one, two, three. "Paintercounts" and "cebwobs" and allergy to tea.

Baby Marion was showered with gifts from our many friends and relations. Christmas, only a few months later, producing yet more presents. Some, such as her engraved sterling silver serviette ring from my "wiggy" aunt, have been treasured forever. Mrs Landon, my old boyfriend Nick's mother, sent me a cut-out baby gown in Viyella that I lovingly hand stitched. Later she sent me a Baby Book. I bought the same type, colour coded for each of my children. I kept a detailed monthly record with photos for their first two years, then three monthly until they were five. Subsequently, I kept a record of their progress until they left school. The Viyella gown is kept as an heirloom with the christening dress and exquisite yellow lacy coat and bonnet set knitted by neighbour Vi. I always kept in touch with the Landons as they had been so kind to me on my wedding day. I stayed with them the previous day as Mrs Landon said, "A girl can't get married from a bed sitting room with no one fussing around her!"

How I enjoyed those early years of motherhood. I always possessed a strong maternal instinct and loved the years when I cared for the little ones whilst doing my two years Nursery Nurses training. Now I had a baby of my very own. I found the responsibility and emotional involvement was very different, but also more satisfying.

A huge disappointment was my inability to breast feed after the first few weeks, as I developed a painful abscess. I soon accepted that Marion could thrive on the formula "Ostermilk" recommended by the Clinic nurse.

Every fortnight I tucked the baby in her pram to visit this "guardian angel." Down the hill I wheeled her to the clinic at the local Parish Hall. Marion thrived and progressed at a normal rate. She gave us a bout of concern with nightly screaming, which was possibly the infamous "three month colic". Mostly she smiled contentedly and her devoted companion was our fluffy, tabby cat Timmy.

No convenient "Baby-gro" all in one outfits for babies in those days. She had a garment that resembled a long, cosy dressing gown that buttoned over at the bottom to form a bag. I dressed Marion in this, tucked her in her pram and outside she went for her morning and afternoon nap in all weathers except actual rain or snow. The moving branches of the old oak tree fascinated and hypnotised her. Later, when she could sit up, she loved watching the occasional car pass or to wave to a friendly passer-by. She was a dear little baby, very much loved.

Crawling and walking at the average age, she showed delight in music when very young. She vigorously conducted the radio. Her independent spirit was obvious from a very young age. She insisted on feeding herself, albeit messily, and deliberately repeated an action when told firmly "No".

By the age of two her speech and imagination were developing fast, as was her sense of humour . . .

Little Miss Muffet sat on her tuffet
Eating her curds away,
. . . Along came a blackbird and pecked off her nose. (giggle giggle,)
or

Little Boy Blue come blow up your horn,
The sheep's in the meadow, the cow's in the corner,
or

Humpty Dumpty sat on a wall,
Humpty Dumpty had a great fall
He stepped in a puddle right up to his middle
And never went there again.

Before Marion was two, I had successfully taught her to blow her nose when I held a hanky to it and invited "blow". For her second birthday I had iced a cake with pink icing and lit the two candles.

She gazed entranced, never having seen flickering flames before. When I said "blow" you can guess what happened!

My next pregnancy followed a similar pattern to the first, with my aversion to tea and early morning sickness that progressed to constant nausea, not much fun. Still, I was absolutely delighted to be expecting another baby as I had always dreaded the thought of an only child. For some reason Don dreaded the idea of twins. Fortunately it did not prove a problem to us, although I discovered later that my grandfather (the one who was corsetière to King Edward VII) was one of identical twins.

The maternity hospital places were limited, so provided no complications were expected, second and third babies were delivered at home with the midwife in attendance. First, fourth and subsequent births were in hospital. This arrangement delighted me as we had no relations who could have cared for two-year-old Marion. I received regular visits from Nurse Scott the midwife.

Marion had been born a week early, the day after a rare outing to Southend. Caroline arrived a week late, but sure enough, the day after a Southend visit, I went into labour. Alas, familiar Nurse Scott was on holiday so the relief nurse, Nurse Lee attended me. Timmy the cat supervised the whole procedure from the top of the wardrobe. Maybe that initial experience influenced Caroline's love of cats.

"You have another lovely little girl," announced Nurse Lee to my joy. She later contacted the doctor to stitch me and check the afterbirth.

The following morning Marion came into the bedroom to discover a new baby sister tucked up in the cot. She was delighted.

All was well for a day or two. I then felt distinctly unwell and developed a high fever that progressed until I was having rigours. The midwife looked at me aghast during her routine visit and immediately went out to the phone box to contact my doctor. As soon as he came he said, "Nurse, phone for an ambulance *immediately* and get Mrs Day admitted to St John's Hospital at Chelmsford."

I can remember little about the bumpy ride there. They admitted me two days prior to Christmas with the unromantic diagnosis of "retained products". (Some of the afterbirth had been retained and was deteriorating inside me. The baby had arrived normally but left some of her "luggage" behind.) My fever prevented me being admitted to a maternity ward so I was sent to Isolation. All the other patients had been discharged for the Christmas holiday, so I was alone, but felt too ill to care.

A minor operation soon had me feeling considerably better. The baby was with me and I was able to continue feeding her. On Christmas Day, Don and Marion travelled the twelve miles by taxi and spent some time with us. The nurses gave Marion the fairy doll from the Christmas tree that had been decorated solely for my benefit.

I made a speedy recovery and they discharged me after a couple of days. I settled down to enjoy my little family.

At birth Caroline weighed 6 lbs, the same as Marion, but stayed very petite all her childhood. She was a loving baby and, unlike her sister, wanted cuddles *all* the time. No baby carriers existed then, so I cut two holes in an army haversack for her little legs and did the ironing or vacuuming with her strapped close to me; fortunately she was a lightweight baby. Caroline made her first intelligible sound at nine months calling Timmy with "ti-ti". Soon afterwards she could say a few basic words, speaking and walking early. "Marion" proved a difficult word for her initially so she substituted "Man-man". I successfully breastfed her until her final feed on her first birthday. She only had one tooth then; had she cut one opposite, I would have stopped earlier.

She was aware of her charm very young, "flirting" with bus conductors and tradesmen, greeting them with "Hallo man." If I called her when she was "helping" Don she said, "Go away, go and cook the dinner."

She played complicated imaginary games, "lifting" sweets off an advertisement and painstakingly unwrapping each one before "eating" it.

"Mummy, please help me put the 'paintercount' on the bed."

Her speech was full of unintentional spoonerisms.

"Look at the big 'cebwob' that spider has made."

"I wish I could have a 'tony pail' like Man-man."

" 'Forn Clakes' are my favourite breakfast."

"A cup of tea is best, but sometimes I like a 'drilky mink'."

Caroline was a small, energetic child with a good appetite. She loved pretty clothes and dressing up and was a darling, sunny-natured toddler.

She loved to "help" and happily dusted or rolled out the pastry. She had her own little shopping basket in which she helped to carry the shopping home. She would have liked to help with the ironing but was too small and I was very aware of the danger of hot irons. Frequently I ironed *inside* the playpen while the children played in the room. They loved the playpen when they were toddlers. I always put in different "surprise" toys to interest them. Wooden spoons, metal baking trays, threaded wooden cotton reels, as well as their favourite conventional toys.

A few years later, once again tea tasted horrible and I knew another baby was on its way. This time the nausea was not quite as bad and I coped without any tablets. Some years earlier, when I was expecting Marion, a common antidote for pregnancy nausea had been Thalidomide. Too late they discovered the frightening deformities it caused to the babies. A little girl locally was born with no arm and her deformed hand attached to her shoulder. I did suffer mild anaemia and the doctor prescribed iron tablets.

"Are they to help you do the ironing?" suggested Caroline.

On June 1st, it was Monday, Marion was at school and I waited at the bus stop with Caroline after my weekly visit to Nickey. I felt some distinctive pains. My baby was not due for another week but was obviously impatient to arrive. Soon after, I realised I was definitely in labour so, as planned, I left Caroline with a neighbour who also took care of Marion on her return from school. Someone was in the telephone box for what seemed like an eternity. Eventually I 'phoned for the ambulance. My bag was packed in readiness and I left a note for Don.

They took me to St Andrew's Hospital at Billericay. It was an uncomplicated delivery and Oliver arrived at eight o'clock like both of his sisters, just as the day and night staff changed shifts. He weighed 6 lbs 6 ozs.

Don came home and before collecting the girls hurried straight to the 'phone box to enquire about my progress. He 'phoned the hospital just as I was being wheeled back to the ward after the delivery.

"I'm enquiring about Mrs Eve Day," he said.

"Here she is," the Sister handed me the telephone and I was able to give him the news first hand.

"We have a baby boy."

After the trauma of Caroline's birth, all had been straightforward. I can honestly say that neither Don nor I were concerned what sex our babies were. We would have welcomed three girls or three boys but now we were delighted to have a little son.

The following day I was discharged as there were no complications. The ambulance returned me just as the main race of the Derby was being shown on television. The triumphant entry I had imagined was eclipsed by Don being absorbed in a far more compelling event. I don't know if he backed a winner that day, but I was happy to be home and introduce Oliver to an excited Caroline and later Marion.

I had what was termed a "short stay" in hospital and was sent home with help supplied by the local council. Don took the girls to Nickey each day whilst he was at work. Soon I was able to return the compliment she had paid me, asking me to be little Elaine's godmother. She was Oliver's godmother and I still have the much used and cherished engraved silver spoon she gave him. It is smaller than a dessertspoon but larger than a teaspoon, a most unusual size, always known as "the big-little spoon".

He was a dear little baby, adored by his big sisters as well as his doting parents.

Choosing names had been a big decision. Having such an exceedingly short name myself, we felt two names of three syllables sounded rhythmical with "Day". Marion's second name was Winifred after Don's sister. Caroline's was Rosemary after my favourite doll and Oliver had Jonathan, in case he disliked Oliver later.

Our little family was now complete with three healthy children to nurture and enjoy.

CHAPTER
EIGHT

Fire

Poor Don was in agony when he trod on a nail. The roof caught fire, but soon was quenched. He loved to tell the tale.

We had decided to add another bedroom on to our small bungalow and were fortunate to have plenty of land at the side. Planning permission eventually granted, we hired a firm of builders to build a room with a door leading from our dining room.

They arrived early each morning. In spite of the inclement weather, varying between rain and snow with a few frosty days of respite, they made good progress. Inevitably bits of building equipment and pieces of wood were left around.

A few days after a heavy snowfall, Don had taken out the coal scuttle to fill it from the bunker adjacent to the house.

"Oooow!" I heard this terrible yell and a crash as the scuttle clattered to the ground. I ran out to see what had caused the disturbance to find Don in agony. The poor man had trodden on a large nail, invisible in a piece of wood under the snow. It went in so deeply that the wound could be seen on the top of his foot. I phoned the doctor who came immediately. He gave an anti-tetanus injection, dressed the wound and prescribed penicillin tablets. He visited Don daily. He was completely incapacitated, only able to sit in the armchair with his foot on a stool.

Soon after we had another heavy fall of snow. When the weak sun shimmered on the glistening branches, it resembled a Christmas card — really magic.

"Mummy, Mummy, can we go out and play in the snow?"

"Later on," I promised. "I have to go down to the shops on the bike for a few things, remember Auntie Win and Uncle Will are coming tomorrow."

I had made a chocolate cake for the event. Never a confident cook, I was relieved that it looked all right. I left it cooling on the rack.

"You're not going on your bike, are you?" called Don, "the roads are far too icy."

I decided to wait for the bus. The children stayed with Don, Marion happily drawing, Caroline in the playpen.

"I won't be long, be good for Daddy."

I saw the bus coming down the hill and just managed to catch it, little knowing that within minutes the house would be on fire.

In England at that time it was the practise to place insulation material under the tiles. This was a bitumen-based product with aluminium facing. It needed a blow torch to give it pliability. Unfortunately the roofing plumber must have been over-enthusiastic and this highly flammable material burned rapidly throughout the ceiling area of the bungalow. We had a common roof with our neighbours so there was the danger of it spreading to their home too.

Don sat in his chair quite helpless as dramatic smoke billowed from the roof. I was happily shopping completely unaware of the drama at home.

Fortunately the carpenter and his lad were also there and acted speedily. They rushed in and out of the house with buckets of water and managed to quench the fire.

We had no serious damage and we were insured. Suitcases with my old school books and boxes of Don's memorabilia had been stored in the attic and were all water-damaged. We just counted our blessings that no one was hurt.

Sadly, in the panic, my lovely chocolate cake was damaged, the least of our worries. I patched it with some icing and when Win and Will arrived the following day, we regaled them with the drama of the fire.

CHAPTER NINE

Aladdin

*Off to see Aladdin, to London on the train Caroline
went happily, Don searched for her in vain.*

One day, after taking Marion to school and returning
home with three-year-old Caroline and baby Oliver, we
settled down to a day of normal domesticity. The
doorbell rang. I never had early morning visitors, yet
there stood elderly Mrs Richards from next door but
one.

"Oh, I'm so glad you're home with Caroline, I
wonder if we could borrow her?"

What a peculiar request, but I invited her in for more
details. She explained —

"Jim and I were taking our grandaughter Alison out
for her birthday today and she has developed
chickenpox. We have managed to get matinée tickets for
the Palladium in London to see Cliff Richards in
'Aladdin'. Would Caroline like to come with us
instead?"

Caroline only knew Mr and Mrs Richards on "hallo"
terms if we passed them in their garden, but she was a
very sociable little girl.

"Would you like to go out with Mr and Mrs Richards on the train to London to a real theatre?" I asked.

"Oh, yes *please!*" she answered, jumping up and down in excitement. She knew about trains but had no idea about the word "theatre".

"Bring her to the station for the five past twelve train then."

Mrs Richards waved goodbye, happy that the ticket would not be wasted.

I had polished Caroline's red shoes and she looked sweet in her pink hat and coat and red gloves. Pantomime time is always in the winter. I kept answering Caroline's pleas of, "Isn't it time to go yet?" and we finally set off for the walk to the station. Oliver had his morning nap as I pushed the pram down the hill.

"Marion won't know where I am," she said. She missed the company of her big sister, now at school.

"Only another week until she breaks up," I consoled her.

Always literal, she looked incredulous and gasped aghast, "Will it hurt her, when she breaks up, will she be able to walk?"

We left in plenty of time and were nearly at the station when I realised she would have had no lunch. Whatever could I do now? Hastily we visited the baker's shop.

"You can choose a bun," I told her.

"Can I eat it *now?*" she asked amazed.

Normally eating in the street was something no nicely mannered child would dream of doing and I had instilled in mine *always* to wait until we were home to have that cake or piece of fruit. That day the rule was broken and she ate the bun as we hurried for the train. I wiped her face and she departed happily with Mr and Mrs Richards.

After a normal afternoon, I collected Marion from the bus and cooked our meal. Don arrived home from work at the usual time expecting to be greeted by his two little daughters. Only Marion was there and I had told her to keep it a secret for a while about Caroline's whereabouts.

"All right, Caroline, where are you hiding?"

Don peered behind the doors and lifted up the long curtains, a favourite hiding place.

"She is not here," I told him, "she has gone to London."

"Oh yes," replied Don, "pull the other leg, it's got bells on."

"She really *has*, Daddy," Marion could contain herself no longer. "She has gone to see Cliff Richards in Aladdin."

Don's jaw dropped. He sat down in amazement as I told him the story.

Soon afterwards Mr and Mrs Richards delivered a very excited and tired little girl home.

"Did you enjoy yourself?" I asked.

"Oh *yes*, there were dancing ladies and men with towels on their bottoms." (loincloths)

From that day she was a great admirer of Cliff Richards (purely coincidental the same name as her benefactors). She delighted in being told again and again how Don had searched for her and didn't believe she was in London, but the biggest thrill that day was being allowed to eat a bun in the street.

CHAPTER
TEN

Caroline's Conquests

Caroline is fickle, which man will she marry?
Mr Biss the shopkeeper, or dear old Uncle Harry?

Now that I had two little girls to clothe as well as myself, I realised it was time I learned the basics of dressmaking. Each Wednesday evening, I cycled across town to evening classes. Later I learnt cookery at the same venue. I can still hear him now, the cookery teacher who made us mix everything by hand, literally, for he despised kitchen tools. We creamed cake mixture rotating our reluctant hands.

"Do not be afeared, ze mixtyur vill not biete you."

I was glad to use the utilitarian sewing machines provided instead of my temperamental "monster" that terrified me. The classes were well run and I soon learned the essential techniques. My first ambitious project, a zip-up snow suit and fur-edged hat for Marion, proved to be a great success. This garment, as with most of her clothes, was eventually worn by a delighted Caroline and later Oliver.

Caroline was a different child from our quiet Marion; she was affectionate, outgoing and a deliberate charmer. She had beguiled the manager of the local Co-op grocery store with her sweetest smile. Mr Biss, a middle aged widower, gave her an occasional sweet when we were shopping. He became her great hero when he presented her with a Christmas stocking filled with chocolate bars.

"I'm going to marry you, Mr Biss."

Little Caroline gave him a big hug as she made this announcement.

One of the students at the dressmaking classes was named Mary Biss.

"Are you any relation to Mr Biss the Co-op manager?" I asked.

"Yes, I'm his daughter," she replied.

"Oh, my daughter is going to marry him."

Mary was most mystified at this woman in her early thirties having a marriageable daughter. She knew her father was an eligible widower and questioned this disconcerted man when she returned home. To her relief, he explained all.

My beloved, eccentric Uncle Harry visited us from time to time. He loved children and Caroline enjoyed a cuddle in bed with him in the mornings. This of course was totally innocent, but sadly today would be viewed with grave suspicion. She had always been going to marry him until her "affair" with Mr Biss. During his next visit, she heartlessly informed him, "I'm not going to marry you now. I'm going to marry Mr Biss."

Poor Uncle Harry! He managed to cope with his rejection and on his next visit even brought her a watch in a box, her first one. The label had written on it "To my ex-fiancée, love Uncle Harry." I believe she still has the box as a keepsake.

He had never married but not from lack of eager and devoted lady friends. One Christmas time he stayed with us and on Boxing Day afternoon announced suddenly "Ah well, I must find out the time of the next train as I am taking a "little gel" to a dance this evening." At that time he must have been nearly eighty as probably also was his "little gel".

We never knew how long he was staying until his announcement of departure. Often he took a stroll along the road in the morning clad in dressing gown and slippers, to the children's great embarrassment. He loved to tell us stories of his adventurous past, again and again and *again*. We never allowed the children to leave the dinner table until everyone had finished. He had the habit of leaving some dessert on his plate, often his favourite "treacly tart" that I had made in his honour. He rambled on and on.

"Did I ever tell you of the time I was a professional roller skater?" he asked.

"Yes," we chorused.

Undaunted, he proceeded to tell the long-winded tale as the children wriggled and fidgeted. He was always very generous, although in his latter years he had very little money. He still lived as in the days when he could have afforded whatever he desired. He loved taking the children to the toyshop and magnanimously ask them "What would you like?"

I had already explained to them quietly before his arrival that the toy must be a modestly priced one, not a bicycle or a doll's pram. They were very understanding and always delighted and grateful for the gifts he bought them.

I have taken after him, liking gimmicky toys. Once he bought the family a model of two Scottie dogs whose eyes lit up. I believe it was a promotion for "Black and White Whisky". In a parcel, he sent a dog that moved and barked. The disconcerted postman delivering this must have accidentally activated the battery switch.

The town greengrocer was a fearsome looking man with half his teeth missing. George however had a very soft heart. He greeted his small customers with "Come over 'ere, I'll smash yer face in," and promptly let them choose an apple or banana. Marion, much shyer was very wary, but Caroline loved him and always begged "Can we go and buy some fruit at 'smash your face in'?"

Not only the men were beguiled by her charm, the lady in the bakery always said. "Come here, little love, choose which bun you would like."

This was then placed in a bag and tenderly carried home by a delighted and delightful little girl.

CHAPTER
ELEVEN

Market Day

Bargains at the market, I loved the atmosphere.
TV with the children, and trips to Southend pier.

I attended the local Catholic church, cycling there each Sunday morning. Near us, in a bungalow similar to ours, lived Olive, also a Catholic, and her husband Bas. I remember her shock one day late in October when I told her proudly that we had a baby daughter. A few days prior to the birth I had cycled to Mass. I wore a loose coat as was the fashion then. It was autumn and no one was aware I was pregnant. With none of my children did my "bump" grow bigger than my then quite modest bustline (probably the advantage of having big hips).

One Sunday Father Collings asked for volunteers for a big spring clean of the church prior to the Bishop's annual visit. I joined some other ladies sweeping and polishing the pews. Caroline lay contentedly in her pram and toddler Marion played with an angelic looking, curly haired, little cherub. I had often admired this little boy's looks at Mass. Now I asked his mother, "What is your delightful little son called?"

"Adam," she answered.

"At last," I replied delightedly, "Eve has found her Adam!"

Later, at the mature age of four he proposed to Marion. She married many years ago but Adam remains a bachelor, maybe he is still waiting for her?

I became very friendly with his mother Nickey, who also had a lovely little auburn haired daughter Kathryn. She was heavily pregnant with her third child.

We lived on opposite sides of the town, but enjoyed a social chat and the children played well together. Monday was Market Day in Wickford. In those days it was split into two venues. The livestock market with the small animals and fowl was on one side of the road and the stalls on the other. Many bargains of fruit, vegetables and eggs were available from folk who had local smallholdings.

Reasonably priced clothing and other items were also for sale. A popular stop was the "knicker man" whose stall displayed a multitude of knickers for adults and children, often "seconds" of well-known brands.

Once Marion was with me, "Mummy, Mummy, I need new navy blue knickers for school," she insisted.

I was looking at cut price cleaning materials.

"Afterwards," I promised. I purchased my soap flakes to be asked, "Is it afterwards *now*?"

Nickey and I both liked looking around the markets unfettered by small children. We developed a routine. She lived a short way up the hill but quite close to the shops. Each Monday I walked the couple of miles to her home and had coffee with her. She had a big

56

garden with the added attraction of the railway at the rear. The children loved to watch the "puffer trains" from the back fence.

"Remember to bring the 'binoculators'," Marion reminded me.

We alternated which one of us went to the market in the morning and which one of us prepared lunch. This never varied, always fish fingers and baked beans. Then the other one went in the afternoon.

Nickey's second daughter Elaine was duly born and I was privileged to be invited to become her godmother, my first godchild. Later Nickey cleverly produced another son Dominic, giving them to my mind the perfect family of two girls and two boys.

Brian her husband was a very kind man and loved children. As a child Nickey had suffered from kyphosis, leaving her with a mildly deformed back. She didn't grumble about it, although she was often in considerable pain, aggravated by walking.

The seaside town of Southend was twelve miles away and famous for its illuminations and its mile-long pier, the longest in the world. Don has never enjoyed sightseeing and we had no car. Each autumn Brian took me and five excited children into his car and off we went for an evening of fun.

The whole Promenade by the sea front was ablaze with myriads of colourful moving tableaux. The illuminations lit the whole length of the pier too. I remember Peter Pan, Pinocchio, Hawaiian dancers and many other fascinating displays. The children were all entranced.

Indulgent Brian had only to hear Kathryn say "Ooo Daddy, *that* smells nice!" as we passed the candy floss and soon we all had our faces immersed in the velvety cushion of pink fluff. The evening concluded with fish and chips eaten out of the newspaper, sitting on a bench by the pier. Caroline had two chips not separated.

"Look, Mummy, I've got semi-detached chips."

Each Sunday when I was expecting my third baby and after, Brian kindly collected us for Mass, travelling quite a few miles out of his way. The children always bought their weekly sweets on the way home.

Adam and Marion went through a phase of wanting Goldilocks for their bedtime story, read from the Ladybird series. Heaven help us if we missed a word. I am sure they both knew it by heart, as Nickey and I did. On Monday we compared notes. "I've got it down to six and a half minutes," she announced triumphantly whereas my score was seven and a half.

Both families delighted in "Watch with Mother" on the television each day. We were usually all together for "Picture Book" on Mondays. Tuesday was the winsome puppet "Andy Pandy". Wednesday "Billanpots" (Caroline's name for Bill and Ben the Flowerpot Men and their irritating little friend "Weeeeed".) and "Rag, Tag and Bobtail" every Thursday. Friday was *my* favourite: "The Woodentops" — "Mummy Woodentop, Daddy Woodentop, Willy and Jenny the twins, and the biggest spotty dog you ever did see". The children all learned the days of the week easily by being aware of the sequence of these programmes.

They loved some of the popular songs of the time such as

Maizy doats and dozy doats and liddle lambsy divy
   A kidly divy too, wooden you

or

It was an itsy bitsy, teenie weenie, yellow polka
   dot bikini
That she wore for the first time today
It was an itsy bitsy, teenie weenie, yellow polka dot
   bikini
So in the water she wanted to stay.

We were very sad when a few years later Nickey and family moved twelve miles away to a lovely home in Brentwood. We visited them occasionally, but always remembered with nostalgia those "market days" when the children were small.

CHAPTER
TWELVE

The 'onest
Woman's 'at

Off to Chelmsford market for the 'onest woman's 'at,
A cup of tea, then find a plastic "mummy pig" that's fat.

One cold, frosty January morning, Don had left for his walk through the white lace-tipped fields to the station and ultimately to work. Marion, aged nine and very competent, had her school satchel ready, complete with "play lunch".

"Oh good, it is Wednesday today, we might be having shepherds pie for school dinner."

When I married, I had to promise Don never to give him minced meat in any form, so this was a treat for my children.

Early in October, Marion had come home worried.

"Mummy, Mrs Callaghan says we must remember our 'plorvers' tomorrow."

Mystified, we phoned her friend Susan's mother to realise that her teacher with a strong Irish accent, was reminding them that they needed their pullovers.

Caroline was very excited as she was going straight from school to her friend Joanne's party "Mummy, mummy, where is the present we wrapped up yesterday? Will she like her card with the big gold 'seven' on it? Should we have bought the red pencil case instead the pink one?"

She hopped from one leg to the other.

The girls looked very smart in their grey pleated skirts and scarlet pullovers. Hurriedly they donned their navy blue gaberdine mackintoshes and scarlet school hats.

"Come on," I said. "I'll see you on to the bus."

The stop was not far from our gate and Oliver, aged three and a half, trotted along with us to wave goodbye to his sisters. He always referred to them as "my children", asking me plaintively each afternoon, "Is it time yet for my children to come home?"

He had been late to talk as a baby, but I was fascinated that his first intelligible sound was "Brmm Brmm", very masculine! He said mummy, daddy and a few simple isolated words. Just before his second birthday, as we looked out of his upstairs bedroom window, he gazed in delight at the large vehicle lumbering along the road, heading for the fields.

"Ooo, combine 'arvester," he said.

He *loved* big words and always used them correctly (and rather precociously). Shapes fascinated him. He could name the obvious circles, triangles and squares but I explained to him that a parallelogram was a rectangle with sloping sides. He loved that word.

61

"Parallel means the lines never meet, they go on for ever."

"How long *is* ever?" he asked. He had a very enquiring mind and often asked similar unanswerable questions such as "Do spiders suck their thumbs? "Does the mummy bird kiss the baby birds goodnight?" "Does God love witches?"

That morning after the girls had left I had a few chores to do before going out. No plastic dustbin or bin liners then. I used sheets of newspaper inside the galvanised bin. Oliver saw me heading outside with newspapers under my arm. He was at the age when he followed me everywhere.

"Where are you going Mummy? What are you doing?"

"I am just going to line the dustbin," I answered.

Horror on his little face, real concern.

"Oh Mummy, what are you going to lie in the dustbin for?!"

After a few explanations I said "Guess where we are going today?"

"To the shops?" he asked eagerly. Any outing anywhere was quite an excitement.

"Well, sort of," I replied. "We're going to Chelmsford markets."

"Ooo-ooo, on the *big* bus," he squealed. "A long bus ride, can we go upstairs?"

"Yes," I agreed, "but let's hurry, the bus leaves in ten minutes."

The drive through the rural countryside and villages seemed so peaceful. The chilly wind had prevented the frost from thawing the stubble in the fields. They looked as if icing sugar had been liberally sprinkled over them. On the outskirts of the lovely old city of Chelmsford, we encountered red traffic lights. Many years previously, when the girls were irritated by the delay I suggested that if they blew hard, the lights would turn green and we could go. It worked every time! Oliver knew this and successfully huffed and puffed. Later the children used to delight in singing the monotonous chant from Monty Python.

I like traffic lights, I like traffic lights, I like
    traffic lights
That is what I said
I like traffic lights, I like traffic lights, I like traffic
    lights
But not when they are red.

The market was already bustling with folk who had arrived by lorry, car, train or bus. We were well wrapped up in winter coats, scarves and gloves. One of my purchases that day was to be a new winter hat. Oliver kept hold of my hand tightly in the throng of people. He was always very good on these occasions as he knew the promised reward would be a new farm animal to add to the family's large collection.

"Can I get a fat mummy pig?" he begged.

"Come on, lidies, loverly 'ats, all sorts, keep yer warm these chilly mornin's, only five bob."

I headed off for the stall and tried on a few hats. One was a velvet and fur fabric Cossack style, another a woollen tweed one with a small brim. I procrastinated. Finally I decided on the tweed one and proffered the Cockney stall holder a ten shilling note. A lady was enquiring about a hat hanging on the awning above the stall.

"Orl right, darlin'," he said, "'alf a mo, an' I'll get it darn."

Temporarily distracted, he put my hat in a bag and gave me fifteen shillings change.

"Excuse me," I said, "you've given me the wrong change."

His cheery face clouded over immediately. Aggressively he muttered "No, I didn't, missus."

"You *did*," I insisted and handed him back the ten shilling note. His face was transformed in an instant. "You gave me change for a pound and I only gave you ten shillings."

He took the note beaming and bellowing at the top of his voice announced

"Oi, lidies an' gents, come 'ere, come an' look at 'er. We got an 'onest woman 'ere, a real 'onest woman."

I felt acutely embarrassed and tried to sidle away.

"Look, lidy," he said, "any 'at on my stall an' it's yours, a present from me."

So, I got my Cossack hat as well.

"I'm thirsty." Oliver, who had been bewildered by the commotion, reminded me of the promised drink-in-a-shop, a real treat.

We walked into the town past a department store with dummies in the window awaiting their garments.

"Look at all the 'nobodies'," was Oliver's pertinent remark.

We passed a toy shop and he was able to choose his "mummy pig", then we stopped at a small café in a side road. He always chose milk.

"I'd like one glass of milk, a pot of tea and two scones please."

The waitress was starting to prepare the tables for lunch and placed condiments and a bottle of H.P. and tomato sauce on each table. Oliver couldn't resist the temptation, he *loved* tomato sauce and tried to shake some on his buttered scone!

"Mummy," he complained as he shook the bottle vigorously, "it hasn't got no nothing in it."

(A *triple* negative, aptly describing "empty".) It was replaced and a happy little boy enjoyed his unconventional scone.

When Oliver was a teenager he went through a phase of collecting hats; he had an air force hat, a sailor's hat, a Sherlock Holmes hat and many others, but his great pride was the 'onest woman's 'at.

CHAPTER
THIRTEEN

A Good Deed

*Two little girls I cared for, while Eileen had
another. Each day a fresh disaster, but I never told
their mother.*

A few months after the birth of Oliver, Marion changed
schools. She had only been at St Helen's in Brentwood
for a year. I took her into Wickford each day where she
met my friend Nickey's two eldest children, Kathryn
aged seven and Adam five. They travelled the twelve
miles on public transport, very competently. Marion's
first teacher's pertinent name was Mrs Boss, a kindly
lady who encouraged her pupil's individuality. That first
Christmas, Marion had the great responsibility of a
speaking part in the Nativity play as the Innkeeper.

"No room, no room."

She practised constantly in case she forgot her lines.

"Mummy, where is Orientar?" She asked concentrat-
ing on a new word. "Is it where the three kings lived?"

A year later a new Catholic school opened in
Basildon only six miles away. This was named after one
of the Forty Martyrs of England and Wales, Blessed
Anne Line, who was martyred in 1601 for harbouring

priests. (The martyrs have since been canonised and the school is now known as St Anne Line's.) A special bus collected the children from neighbouring towns.

On her first day at this new school, Marion looked very smart in her scarlet uniform. I waved goodbye as she mounted the bus.

"Have a lovely day, I'll be here to meet you this afternoon."

A heavily pregnant lady was also waving goodbye to her little girl on her very first day at school.

"Now you be a good girl and do what the teacher tells you."

Like me she also had a daughter of three and a half. I chatted to Eileen who had recently moved to Wickford. Later, over a cup of tea she told me her story. Originally from Ireland and a qualified nurse, she had worked for many years both in England and abroad. She had married Peter later in life. Their first baby, a little boy, had Down's Syndrome and severe heart problems. He had died only the previous year, aged five, and she was still coming to terms with the sad loss. I gathered that all her time had revolved around Matthew. The two little girls, Anne-Marie and Fiona, although not neglected, had not been able to have a lot of quality time spent with them. She knew nobody in the area and told me her two daughters would need to go to a Residential Children's Home when she went to hospital for the imminent usual ten days confinement.

I felt so grateful to have been blessed with three normal, healthy children. I went home and asked Don,

"How would you feel if we had two little girls to stay for just ten days while their mother is in hospital?"

He was a bit surprised at this request as our bungalow was quite small and he wondered how we would accommodate them.

"They will bring their own folding beds and Oliver's cot can come into our bedroom," I suggested.

"All right, it is up to you, you will be the one coping."

Eileen was very relieved to know they would be in a home, not a "Home".

Her very first day at school, mischievous Anne-Marie quietly entered each of the girls' lavatories, locked them from the inside and crawled out under the gap in the door. This caused a mighty uproar as little girls battered on the doors trying to get in. The result, apart from being chaotic, resulted in a few unexpected puddles and tears from these little five-year-olds on their first day at school. Every few days, Marion would recite the latest horrific story of Anne-Marie's misdeeds. I should have been warned!

The day soon arrived when Eileen went into labour. Peter brought the beds and we just managed to fit them into baby Oliver's small, newly decorated bedroom. I took a deep breath, hoped for the best and reminded myself it was only for ten days. Little did I know!

The second morning when I went in to awaken them, I found that Fiona had happily and painstakingly picked long strips off the new wallpaper. The following day, she put the plug in the bathroom hand basin and left the tap on, flooding the floor. We heated the house with a back boiler and a radiator in each room.

"It's very chilly in here," announced Don as he returned from work having walked through the frosty fields. "Have you had problems with the boiler?"

"Someone" had deliberately gone round and carefully turned each radiator off. Meanwhile, unfortunately Eileen had complications with the birth of her third daughter, Mary-Thérèse. It was with horror that we realised her stay in hospital would definitely be extended.

Fiona fell over and bumped her head causing a large, very obvious, egg-shaped lump on her forehead. This very pretty, innocent looking child then scribbled all over the door with wax crayons before stamping on them and grinding them into the carpet. At every meal one of them spilt their milk or managed to tip food on to the floor.

One evening Anne-Marie said, "I feel poorly, very poorly — oh, oh I'm going to be sick."

Six times that night I got up to her. The poor little girl was too ill to go to school and later that morning developed a blotchy rash. Fiona, not to be outdone, had a massive nosebleed and that evening, when I bathed her, I realised that she too was developing a rash.

"Oh no, not measles."

I phoned for the doctor who took one look at them and said, "Scarlatina, nothing to worry about, it is not serious."

Thank God their rashes soon disappeared but not their diabolical behaviour.

Somehow Fiona managed to turn on the *safety* taps on the gas stove, fortunately identified quickly by my sensitive nose. I was still breast feeding five-month-old Oliver; she kicked her slipper in his face. Anne-Marie bit my little Caroline, who had been amazed and in awe of these two naughty girls.

Peter came to our home for meals each weekend. After three very long weeks, Eileen was sufficiently recovered to be discharged from hospital with the baby. We gave a huge sigh of relief when Peter collected the girls and the beds.

Later I was asked to be Mary-Thérèse's godmother, but have not seen her since she was about two. Peter was transferred to the North of England. Eileen and I have always stayed in touch. I visited them some years ago and reminisced on our short friendship. I never worried her with details of the girls' behaviour. All are now happily married with Anne-Marie and Fiona having children of their own. I wonder how they are coping?

CHAPTER
FOURTEEN

The Dentist

New Zealand dentist's family, invite them to our home, Children playing hairdressers, with scissors and a comb.

Our Australian dentist had given me gas for a tooth extraction in 1963. As I recovered the nurse said, "You were mumbling about New Zealand, what a coincidence, we have a New Zealand dentist joining us next week. Mr Hall has decided he needs an assistant in the practice."

My brother David had emigrated there many years previously and was now married with three young boys. At that time we were toying vaguely with the idea of joining him. I was very curious about life in New Zealand.

The following week I went for my check up and met the new dentist. He explained that his parents had emigrated from Finland as I struggled to pronounce his name, George Ruohonen. He told me that he, his wife Joy and little girl Anita, were renting a house off the London Road. This was the opposite side of town to us.

They knew no one in England and were finding everything rather strange.

"Come to tea on Sunday," I said spontaneously and explained that our two daughters were respectively a year older and a year younger than Anita and would enjoy her company. We had no telephone, but he had a car so I gave him our address and directions.

Sunday afternoon, Marion aged five and Caroline three, dressed in matching clothes, eagerly awaited a new little friend. I had been busy baking; shortbread, brandy snaps, chocolate cake, all was ready for our New Zealand visitors. We waited and waited. Eventually Don said, "Blow this for a lark! They're obviously not coming, we may as well have tea."

We did. I felt very disappointed after all the preparations and the enthusiasm with which George had accepted the invitation.

Six o'clock and the girls were in the bath when the doorbell rang. There stood the Ruohonen family. George, his attractive, elegant, young wife Joy and their exquisitely dressed little girl Anita, sporting two long blonde plaits. We greeted them warmly and invited them inside, offering them the remnants of the tea party food.

This was to be the beginning of a life-long friendship. Only after they had returned to New Zealand and we were living in Australia and visiting them, did we discuss our initial meeting. We all had a good laugh.

In England, if someone is invited to "tea", especially on a Sunday, when one would have had a main midday meal, the usual time was mid-afternoon for tea and cakes. In New Zealand (and Australia) "tea" means the main evening meal. Poor George and Joy had arrived at six o'clock probably expecting a pre-prandial drink followed by a meal. What did they get? Chocolate cake! The fact that we are still very close friends is proof of their forgiving nature.

When shopping, Marion always wanted to handle everything. We called her "Felicia Ropps" after the poem by Gellett Burgess which starts

> Funny how Felicia Ropps
> always handles things in shops.

She was a bright, creative little girl who loved making things and drawing, but her great attraction was for scissors. She could not resist cutting things she shouldn't.

My two little girls played hairdressers. Caroline sat happily compliant with a towel around her shoulders whilst Marion brushed and combed her hair. As soon as I was elsewhere, the scissors appeared and Caroline's hair was grabbed in a handful and chopped off; one little girl sporting a dramatic reverse Mohican hairstyle!

Anita Ruohonen's long blonde plaits were her mother's pride. One day I was enjoying a cup of tea with Joy and the three little girls were playing happily in their play room. Suddenly Caroline ran in, "Mummy, Mummy, Marion has cut Anita's hair."

I gasped in horror as I saw Joy's distraught face. We hurried in fearfully, expecting to see Marion triumphantly holding one of Anita's plaits. To my great relief she had only mutilated her neat little fringe. From that moment I confiscated the scissors. Marion probably didn't use them legitimately until her teenage years. She has always been a competent sewer but uses scissors in a very cack-handed manner.

"It's your fault, Mum, you wouldn't let me use them when I was little," she accused me.

Do you blame me?

CHAPTER
FIFTEEN

Holidays

A week away and day trips, Kew was a delight, Don and Bernhard graciously let Marion fly her kite.

When the children were small, we had no vehicle, not a lot of spare money and rarely went on holiday.

Once we went for a week to a holiday camp on the Isle of Sheppey in Kent which none of us really enjoyed. We did not care for the regimentation or mediocre food. The children had their own dining room and Marion was most indignant that they would not give her a cup of tea. All my children had been used to tea from a very young age, often milk with just a dash of tea, but to them it *was* a cup of tea. I always said I weaned them straight from me to tea. In retrospect, I don't know what made us decide on that holiday. I believe a friend had recommended it. Don felt unwell most of the time as he did a few years later when we travelled by coach to St Osyth on the Essex coast.

This small town, adjacent to Clacton, had an interesting history. In Saxon times, the Danes invaded and the prioress was beheaded for refusing the chieftain's advances. Tradition says that a holy well sprung up where her head fell. This became a place of pilgrimage in the Middle Ages. The town was affectionately known as "Toozy" by the natives.

The beautifully manicured Priory grounds were graced by peacocks including an albino. Caroline was so enamoured by the story, that later when she was confirmed, she chose the name "Osyth". The Archbishop officiating thought he had mis-heard.

"Joseph?" he enquired, mystified at a girl taking the name of a male saint.

"No, *Osyth*," she replied.

Being a very learned man he had actually heard of this little known saint.

"So, we have a Saxon maiden here, have we?"

One year, Roy Wiggins, a colleague of Don's at Hackney Tech, made a suggestion.

"We only live a short distance from you, why don't we hire a large eight seater vehicle between our families, I'm happy to drive."

Our girls were five and three, Oliver a babe in arms. Their daughter Eileen was six and little boy Roy nearly three. They had recently moved to Wickford from the East End of London and had definite cockney accents.

Don and Roy decided a week would be all we could afford and plans were made for days' outings. We visited the seaside towns of Clacton and Walton. Twice we went to Bradwell. In spite of being August, the height of summer, it rained both times. The children happily collected shells in their pails in the drizzle. and little Roy was persuaded to dig in the sand, rather than eat it.

76

The weather was hot and humid when it wasn't raining and, with no air conditioning, it was stifling inside the vehicle.

"Eyen't it 'ot in 'ere," proclaimed little Roy with annoying regularity. My two daughters, horrified at his speech, tried to correct him.

"No, Roy," they said, "isn't it *Hot* in *Here*."

Eventually, triumphantly he announced, "Isn't it 'ot in 'ere."

This became a family catch phrase of ours whenever we experience stifling heat. We just say "Little Roy Wiggins", meaning of course "eyen't it 'ot in 'ere".

I had always suffered from travel sickness on boats, buses and cars and had unpleasant nausea most of the time. Poor baby Oliver was sick too a couple of times, not helping matters.

Occasionally we visited Don's sister Win and husband Will. After their West African posting he had retired as a Major. They were now happily settled with their family in Surrey. This was quite an adventure for us as it involved two train journeys and crossing London by Underground. On one of these excursions we saw the famous Zulu, Prince Monolulu, in all his colourful regalia. Caroline smiled at him and they had quite a chat. At the races, he was a well-known tipster with his cry of "I gotta horse".

Will was always referred to as "Wicked Uncle Bill" as he taught Caroline to "blow raspberries" when she was quite tiny. (Only recently did I discover why that rather obscene noise is called a raspberry. It is Cockney rhyming slang for "Raspberry Tart"!) Win was an excellent cook. Unfortunately, she had no idea of time, so that when the delicious lunch was eventually served at three o'clock, we were so desperately hungry we didn't really appreciate her efforts.

Sometimes kind friends or relations would take us out for the day in their car. One day we visited the picturesque town of Maldon, not far away, with the Wilson family. We enjoyed watching the boats in the harbour. At the inlet, Marion leaned over too far and fell in the water. At this stage in our lives none of us could swim. Don managed to grab her hair and haul her out. Once when my cousin Bernhard and wife Vicki took us to Maldon we went for a meal in a very nice hotel. I had taken the girls to the "Ladies" (or lavatory shop as Caroline called it) when she emerged delighted and informed an interested audience in the foyer, "They've got a *pink* lavatory in there."

Small children are usually outspoken and don't know the meaning of tact. Once in our local chemist's shop, Caroline piped in her loud and very clear voice, "Oh Mummy, look at that lady's fat legs."

I could hardly deny the fact when I saw the lady but, trying to distract her, suggested she chose a colour for Daddy's new toothbrush. Not to be silenced, she declared, "Blue, *and* she's got fat arms too."

Bernhard's mother, Aunt Ella and my mother, had been more than just cousins, they had been very close friends. Neither had married until their mid-thirties, very unusual in those days. My parents had an arranged marriage, but I don't know about Aunt Ella and Uncle Arthur. Bernhard, an only child, was the same age as my eldest brother and had spent a lot of his holidays with us. He and wife Vicki, a talented artist, lived a rather insular life. Vicki was quite amazed to realise that one dug potatoes from the ground, and was shocked that we cut off the dead flower heads.

"Oh, the poor things," she exclaimed, but was always delighted to take home a bunch of freshly picked flowers from the garden.

They were always very kind and generous to us. Once, on a visit, they brought the girls each the unlikely gift of a pair of real kid gloves each. (These were probably compulsory attire in Vicki's youth.) Another time they brought a kite. Don and Bernhard had great fun flying it, with the children running after them plaintively crying, "Let *me* have a turn."

When Win and Will went away for a week, we stayed in their home and had a good time going out for days in my familiar Surrey. I was able to visit Dad in Guildford, only half an hour away by train, and dear Diddley, my godmother and her family, in nearby Little Bookham. Hampton Court was only a short bus ride away, a place of endless historical fascination, both the Palace and the magnificent gardens. We strolled through the parklands and gave the children a piece of Fry's "Sandwich" chocolate, which was exceptionally hard. Marion, who must have been about five, grizzled the rest of the afternoon, "That chocolate made my tooth wiggly, oh, oh, my tooth is wiggly."

Of course nature took its course and fortunately the fairies knew she was staying at Auntie Win's.

During the school holidays, once a week we had an outing. Sometimes we took a picnic to a charming park in Billericay, Lake Meadows. This was just a short bus ride. Oliver dawdled as we walked in the park.

"Come on, Oliver," said Marion. "I'm walking on ahead."

"Oh, where's the head you are walking on?" he asked innocently. He always liked to have the last word, even when very small. One day while waiting at the station, he made a lovely malapropism.

"Mummy, which flatporm does the train go from?"

When we all laughed and told him the correct word, his answer was

"Well, it's *flat,* isn't it?"

We regularly went on a day trip by coach to Kew Gardens. Here, Don could indulge in his examination of the many beautiful plants. I loved the variety of things to see; the massive greenhouses with tropical vegetation, the giant water lily and huge pond full of fish and ducks. We always took a bag of bread and were fascinated by the eager, large mouths of the fish awaiting our offering. The ducks were rarely quick enough. The children just loved the freedom of the acres of beautifully mown lawns. We often met Don's colleague Garry, his wife Betty and two little girls Heather and Catherine there. One meeting, when Oliver and Catherine were aged two, she spent hours chasing Oliver to kiss him. He was always popular with the girls.

During the school holidays we went by coach to the ancient city of Colchester where we visited the small zoo. The lasting horrific memory of the place was the eagle being fed dead, yellow, fluffy baby chicks.

Chessington Zoo, originally a large country mansion set in parklands, is now a rather garish Theme Park. Although it was not a large zoo, like my favourite in Regent's Park London, the animals were well housed. We were able to get close to the enclosures. A big attraction of the day was a ride on the little train that circumnavigated the perimeter of the grounds.

Once I took the three children to the Tower of London. Don never liked sightseeing. We saw the Beefeaters in their scarlet uniforms, the traditional ravens and visited the White Tower. Later as we strolled through the Armoury a Guide befriended us.

"Look out of the window," he instructed, "that White Tower was built by William the Conquerer."

Caroline gaped in awe at the thought of such an industrious man.

"What, all by himself?" she gasped.

We *did* have some fun times and many memories remain of exciting and eventful outings.

CHAPTER
SIXTEEN

Runwell Horticultural Show

Domestication flourishing, I'd learned to cook and sew, Don and I won medals and cups at Runwell Show.

When I married I could boil an egg, make tea and open a tin for baked beans on toast. Liver and bacon casserole was the only meal I knew how to prepare.

I thoroughly enjoyed being hurled into unaccustomed domesticity, though found it rather daunting initially. A wedding present from the Ministry of Food staff was, at my request, *The Good Housekeeping Book of Cookery*. (Rather apt, considering the donors!) I was leaving working there so it was also a "farewell" gift. All the contributors signed it and now I read their names nostalgically. This book became my "bible".

At the age of twenty-four I had never used a vacuum cleaner, cleaned a lavatory or even tackled a week's washing. What a lot I had to learn. My mother was long since dead, as also was Don's, so I learned by trial and (lots of) error. My fragmented childhood had denied me the usual household tasks a girl would be expected to perform. These naturally prepared her for marriage or nowadays for independent living. I had done just that for some years before marriage but in a bed-sitting room with very limited facilities. This pattern continued after we were married for a few years, until we moved into our own bungalow.

After Marion's birth I became a full time housewife. Cooking? Don enjoyed very plain traditional English food that I soon learned to cook adequately with the aid of my "bible". I am a person who enjoys experimenting. When I make birthday cards or home-made chocolates, I am prepared to fiddle endlessly. Cooking fancy biscuits, cakes and particularly sweets really appealed to me. Over the years I have had many a disaster and have never been a confident cook. It is fortunate that I have always liked things overcooked. The slightly burned biscuits or cake that went crunchy, I devoured happily. One of our favourite accompaniments to the Christmas meal were tiny sausages wrapped in bacon and grilled on toothpicks. With good reason this tasty snack was referred to as "burnt sticks". The jam turnovers, always rather overdone on the corners, were called "scorchers". I wonder why?

Don loved growing things and by nature and confession was a "park gardener". He liked a rectangular bed or border planted with one or two species as opposed to curved beds and herbaceous borders. He never liked trees, other than his small prolific cordon fruit trees. Trees cut out the sun and dropped branches in high winds. Our tastes in gardens could not be more opposed, but the garden has always been the place Don happily worked in (and swore about!). I have never sat in it, but the children *did* play on the lawn.

A neighbour persuaded Don to join the Runwell Horticultural Society and he happily and successfully competed in the Summer and Autumn Shows. He showed flowers, vegetables and fruit. Boxes of medals and ribbons prove his horticultural ability. His begonias deservedly won the blue ribbon for best exhibit in the Show.

"Oh dear it's raining and that wind is getting vicious, quickly, where are the paper bags?"

Some weeks before the Autumn Show our garden sported a flower bed with chrysanthemums encased in bags to protect the incurve. It was an anxious time hoping the various blooms would be at perfection for *the* day and the vegetables at their peak. Each year, Don became more proficient in the timing of his planting so that, for the Show, the exhibits were in their prime.

The Ladies' Sections (how discriminating!) had many classes; jams, pickles, bottled fruit, scones, cakes, fancy cakes, bread, knitting, needlework and flower arrangements.

Initially I entered the scones and fancy cakes and when I won first prize in both of these, I was encouraged to attempt the other classes. The only one I never attempted was knitting. I am *not* a competitive person, but these shows offered me a challenge to learn to produce more than just essential cookery. As a reward for my efforts, I have two silver cups for the most points in the Ladies' Sections — 1964 and 1965, and the "Woman's Own" diploma for handicrafts for my needlework.

I prepared months in advance, jam making, bottling, embroidering, pickling. I baked the fruit cake the week before and had fun trying elaborate finishes on the fancy cakes. I agonised over the various icings and decorations to make them unique and attractive.

"Has anyone seen the jar of tiny edible silver balls?"

I searched frantically to find them eventually in the toy box.

"We were just playing shops."

The day before the Show was sacrosanct. I concentrated on bread making, praying for warm weather so that I could use the heat of the greenhouse to prove the dough. Eventually I produced two fat, plaited, golden brown, poppy seeded loaves. They looked and smelt irresistible. The best one to exhibit, the other we usually enjoyed as a Pre-Show treat.

Show morning I arose at 6 o'clock and scoured the garden for blooms *not* being exhibited by Don that I could use for the floral arrangement. Don left early taking his collection in a friend's car. They were both on the Committee and helped to prepare the Parish Hall.

I left the children at the hall with my first load, where they "helped" Don. I returned using the invaluable pram to transport my exhibits. Once, disaster struck. The pot of strawberry jam fell over spilling its contents.

"Oh dear, what a mess," I groaned. "What has it damaged?"

Fortunately only two labels on the pickles needed replacing and a bit of first aid was given to the floral arrangement. It took ages to remove all traces of the red glutinous mess from the base of the pram. The wasps were not long in discovering it and I received a painful sting trying to clean up. I remembered the old saying "Bicarb for bees and winegar for wasps," an excellent remedy.

At the Prize Giving, after the cups, medals and certificates had been distributed, most exhibits were auctioned. One year some good friends of ours bought my prize loaf that had been cut in half to verify the texture. Many years later they admitted that it ended up in the dustbin. I had forgotten to add any salt! The children also exhibited successfully. They were busy, demanding, challenging times but very satisfying and worthwhile experiences.

CHAPTER
SEVENTEEN

Happy Days

Children's funny sayings, telling lots of rhymes. Making friends — and pastry. These were happy times.

I took great pride polishing the chrome on my two-tone, big grey pram. The centre lifted out for storage (and for hiding "secrets"). I used a cat net initially as I was concerned that the baby's face could be a nice warm sleeping place for Timmy. It was never necessary.

Marion was just over two years old when Caroline was born, too young to tackle the long walk to the town. I bought a pram seat for her. During the tedious walk to the shops, I recited endless rhymes and poems to them. They loved the rhythm of A.A. Milne's

> The King asked the Queen and the Queen asked
>   the dairymaid,
> "Could we have some butter for the Royal slice
>   of bread?"

The Queen asked the dairymaid, the dairymaid
  said "Certainly,
I'll go and tell the cow now before she goes to
  bed . . ."

or

James, James Morrison Morrison Weatherby
  George Dupree
Took great care of his mother, though he was
  only three.
"James James" said his mother, "Mother" he
  said, said he;
"You must never go down to the end of the town
If you don't go down with me."

I have a pash on Ogden Nash! I love his manipulation
of words. The children loved "Belinda".

Belinda lived in a little white house
With a little black kitten and a little grey mouse,
A little yellow dog and a little red wagon
And a really -o- truly -o- little pet dragon . . .

Marion and I drew a colourful picture of them,
complete with the pirate who appears (and disappears)
later in the poem.

Having a very enquiring mind she wanted to know
the meaning of the word "gyrate" that came later in the
rhyme.

Ink and Blink in glee did gyrate,
around the dragon who ate the pirate.

I explained how it meant to go round and round. She would nearly make herself giddy spinning around shouting "Look, Mummy, I can gyrate."

A large quince tree grew in a well tended garden in Swan Lane. Marion always watched out for it.

"Halfway, Mummy, we're halfway," she proclaimed.

One day when I was wheeling them to the Baby Clinic, I met a lady also heading there with her two little boys. Margaret came from an established Wickford family, her father a prestigious local builder. We struck up a lasting friendship. Paul and Mark were slightly older than my two little girls and they played well together. Margaret and I often shared a pot of tea and a chat at each other's home. Douglas, her husband, was an enthusiastic and knowledgeable gardener like Don and the two families became very close. We had many outings together and they have a good old-fashioned cine film of all the children playing one Christmas. I have always thought of them as very special friends.

Marion had a quaint but logical way with words. Instead of telling me the cup belonged on the hook, she would say "It 'longs to be' on the hook" or when in a vehicle about to overtake another "Are we going to 'take over' that car?" or "You'll have to 'unkey' the door before we can get in."

Caroline took expressions literally.

"Mummy, you said the fire's gone out — where to?"

When she was very small, truth and fiction were all the same as they are with most children. She would tell me amazing stories from her vivid imagination.

"Is that really true?" I asked her. "I can tell, you know, if I look on the tip of your tongue." She clapped her hands over her mouth.

Once she came running in, highly excited, with her tongue hanging out as far as it could.

"Mummy, a car knocked a man on his bike over and he is lying on the road." Yes, it *was* the truth. Luckily the road turned such a sharp corner that vehicles slowed down and no one was seriously hurt.

Those early days with the children were great fun and I thoroughly enjoyed their company and doing lots of activities together. There were no kindergartens or play groups but they socialised with Nickey's and Margaret's children and other little friends.

I designed and Don made "Littlethorne". We lived in "Wildthorne" and this was the children's own "house", not a "Wendy house" or a "Cubby". Basically it was a large hardboard hinged screen, a very simple and effective structure. It folded flat or could be hooked to the corner of the conservatory (or any corner). The outside we painted, inside we wallpapered. An opening door with a real knocker, a "must", was on one side and on the other an opening for a window with curtains that drew. The children felt total privacy once they shut the door and drew the curtains, forgetting that adults could see over the top! Inside it contained no sophisticated furniture. A sturdy laundry box from my single days was a bed. Boxes made chairs with bigger ones covered by a tea towel for a table. Many a doll enjoyed a tea party in there and sometimes an operation.

"Shall we play dolls or hospitals?" suggested Marion, "which?"

"Oh yes," agreed literal Caroline, "Yes, I'll be the witch!"

Over the years we had a number of unconventional parties for the doll's or cat's birthdays. One year Don's vegetable garden was inundated with cabbage white caterpillars.

"Let's have a caterpillar party," I suggested. We made caterpillar invitations for a few of the children's friends. I made a caterpillar cake; even the little iced cakes had green squiggles. We played games such as "Moths and Butterflies" and their wings (arms) were raised above their heads or outstretched just like the relevant insects when they sleep.

They went into the garden and each child collected as many caterpillars as they could in their own jar, a unique competition. We never told them what became of their "treasures". When we played statues Caroline proudly announced "Look, I can stand as still as a soldier in a 'century' box."

When Oliver was small and the girls at school, I fixed a seat on to my bicycle and off we went visiting or to the shops.

Glenn Doman's book "Teach Your Baby to Read' was the latest trend and I was a bit cynical, but thought I would try it. We both thoroughly enjoyed experiment-ing with the suggestions played totally as a game. I held up a card with a word written in large letters, "Table" "Wall" "Mummy" "Biscuit tin". Oliver would then go and touch the article. He could read about forty nouns before he was three. We then acted out the verbs such as "Hop" "Jump" "Whisper". He lost interest soon afterwards and I didn't pursue it. I had no desire to produce a prodigy but it had proved to me that it was definitely possible to recognise words at this young age. Oliver, like his sisters, learned to read easily at school because he was interested, not because of any early influence.

He was a very slim little boy and often wore tightly fitted trousers.

"Shure," said my Irish friend Teresa, "and doesn't his little bottom look loike two eggs toyed in a hanky?"

There were days when the glue pot and scissors appeared, plus the scrapbooks and old magazines. The children had fun cutting and sticking. Colouring books, crayons, paints and other happy diversions amused us on many wet days. The push along train set was a favourite as were the wooden blocks for making roadways for the little car collection, building towers and bridges too.

"Mummy, are you making pastry today?"

No coloured play dough then. Still, after a happy time manipulating (and mutilating) the dough they eventually had the ? pleasure of eating the grey distorted shapes.

The sturdy "baby walker" that Don made was one of their best toys. Caroline fitted into it when it was used as a pram, sometimes it was a cart or a wheelbarrow.

Board games such as the perennial favourites Snakes and Ladders or Ludo were popular as soon as a dice could be read. Later Monopoly became an addiction. We sang songs and chanted endless little rhymes. A favourite song with the nonsense chorus was "The Witch Doctor"!

Ooo ee ooo ah ah, bing bang wallah wallah bing bang
Ooo eee ooo ah ah, bing bang wallah wallah bang *bang*.

A favourite skipping rhyme, complete gibberish —

Eeny meeny mackaracka air i doma nacka chicapocka lolla poppa om pom push!

Children love the rhythm of the words whether they make sense or not.

When I was a little girl, it was instilled in me *always* to write a "thank you" letter for any gift received. I taught the same principle to my children. Christmas brought many parcels and gifts. I hope they learned by example as we all tried to get our letters written by Twelfth Night, January 6th.

I have always been a bibliophile and encouraged the children to enjoy books. The initial introduction to this delight is being read to. They loved A.A. Milne's popular stories of "Winnie-the-Pooh", Kenneth Grahame's "Wind in the Willows" and those of Beatrix Potter, such as "Peter Rabbit". They particularly delighted in

93

the absurdities of Donald Bissett. Don often told them bedtime stories of "Reginald the Forgetful Rabbit".

My original stories *always* started —

"Once-upon-a-time-there-was-a-little-boy-called-John-who-lived- in-a-house-with-his-mummy-and-his-daddy-and-his-baby-brother-Tommy-and-a-little-dog-called-Patch. One day —" all in one breath! I would then use the narrative for all sorts of reasons, maybe to prepare them for a visit to the dentist.

"John sat in a big chair and a nice man in a white coat said 'Open your mouth wide and I will count your teeth,' " or maybe John would visit a big shop to see Father Christmas.

When Caroline was nearly four we went to the large department store in Southend, Keddies. Caroline sat confidently on Father Christmas's lap and whispered something into his ear. I could see him trying to control his laughter. Later he beckoned to me and said, "Over the years I have been asked for all sorts of things, but this one takes the cake."

"Whatever did she want?" I asked with some trepidation.

"A back-scratcher of her very own," he chuckled.

CHAPTER
EIGHTEEN

More Happy Days

Blackberries and bluebells and knickerbocker glories.
Uncle Harry's illness and happy Brownie stories.

The country lanes abounded in bramble hedges and during the season we went armed with paper bags, no plastic then, and collected the delicious ripe blackberries. A small area close to us that not many people knew of once had cultivated bushes. These large choice ones we kept to eat rather than cook. We returned from our forays with purple stained mouths and fingers (and often clothes). Inevitably a few scratches were suffered from the prickly thorns. Don used blackberries to make wine. He was highly successful and used many other fruits and vegetables to produce excellent wines often indistinguishable from the commercial product. Parsnip wine, rhubarb and rose petal — quite delicious, barley, and wallflower were just a few of his triumphs.

A short way up Brock Hill, "Goldilocks Wood", carpeted in bluebells, enticed us during May. We gathered armsful but invariably their drooping stems made them rather unattractive in a vase, they looked far more beautiful growing naturally in the woods.

Nick's brother Ambrose and his wife Margaret lived in a small village in North Essex. They visited us occasionally. We loved to take a couple of buses to their charming bungalow in Cold Norton to visit them. Their children Louise and William played so well with ours and it was a treat to see a friend I had known from my younger days in Guildford.

Mostly, people visited us. Nearly every Sunday, except in mid-winter, Don's relations or friends called in, often en route from the coast. We were always prepared with food in the larder. I loved seeing people and have always been an emotional person who is eager to cling to friendships.

My father had moved into a boarding house in Guildford after my mother's death in 1941 and remained there until well into his eighties. He then moved to another boarding house in Eastbourne to be near his sister, Aunt Bess. I had always referred to her as my "wiggy aunt" because of the obvious yellow wig she always wore. After my mother died when I was eleven, it was she who organised me and my fragmented life and schooling. Now she organised Dad's.

We did see him very occasionally, but he remained a very private and distant man. He had never seen my brother David's three sons, so I felt happy that he had been able to hold Oliver. He died peacefully after lapsing into a coma induced by a massive stroke, in his eighty-sixth year.

Soon after Oliver's birth we received a telegram informing us that Uncle Harry was in St Mark's

Hospital in London with cancer of the bowel. I was his next of kin as David was in New Zealand and cousin Jill in Canada. The staff at St Mark's were very dedicated. This hospital specialised in diseases of the rectum and colon. Initially he was a very sick man, but after the operation his ebullient spirit triumphed and he made a rapid and complete recovery. Whilst in the hospital he charmed all the staff with his cheerfulness and jokes. Whenever Don or I visited him, one of his concerned millionaire friends would be there, such as the President of the British Motor Association or Raymond Way, the motor magnate. Many years later he moved to a bed-sitting room in Brighton where he spent his last years. Sadly he died alone at the ripe old age of eighty-seven. He was an unforgettable, lovable, unique character.

Uncle Harry never married, but a friend's daughter, who had married twice, was asked by a colleague, "Where did you getting your wedding cake made?"

"Oh," she replied "my mother *always* makes my wedding cakes!"

She has since remarried for the third time. I think she must be addicted to wedding cake!

I was very careful not to transfer the brontophobia that I had inherited from my mother to *my* children. Unfortunately, my arachnaphobia could not be concealed. The children too, hated spiders. Once the girls found one on their bedroom windowsill. I had to ask Don to remove it. They refused to go to bed in case there was another spider so I pinned a notice on their door "NO SPIDERS ADMITTED". They went to bed happily.

We bought our first television before Marion was three years old. The first thing we watched was a Rugby match. She looked in horror at the players' muddy knees.

"They have to have a bath" she said with concern.

Like me, she loved pomp and spectacle. The sadness of the day meant nothing to a little girl, but we sat captivated by the splendour of Winston Churchill's funeral. She had sat so still she developed pins and needles in her foot. Always very expressive with her vocabulary she said. "Oh Mummy, it feels as if I have a fizzy drink in my foot."

We loved watching Richard Hearne as "Mr Pastry", Sooty and Sweep, Captain Pugwash and later the exciting Dr Who series. Oliver hid behind the chair so that the Daleks couldn't see him. We also watched the terrible tragedy in 1966 when the school in Wales was demolished by coal waste sliding down a mountain at Aberfan.

Don, who had been in the R.A.F, rarely talked about the war. Oliver overheard him talking of the number of the Lancaster crew to Douglas

". . . we were only seven."

Oliver looked amazed. "Were you only *seven* when you flew in the plane, Daddy?"

Another time when he took Don's remarks literally was one day when we were all out together.

"Daddy, can I have that little car, please buy me that car."

"The last thing I'm buying is toys." replied Don.

"All right," said Oliver, "buy the other things first."

Once we went on a family outing on the train to Southend. The children enjoyed the delight of a knickerbocker glory — a sundae glass containing layers of ice-cream, fruit, cream, sauce and all manner of delectable things. Those were the days when a drink-in-a-shop was a big treat. It was in Sainsbury's there, many years later, that we first saw that wonderful innovation of "magic" (electronic) doors. The children and I must have entered and exited a dozen times. Don stopped at a small hardware shop to buy some seeds. Outside on racks, various small tools were displayed. Oliver, still in his pushchair had helped himself to a small trowel. We were not aware of this until we were on the train home. On our next visit, many months later, Don enquired the price of the trowels.

"Four and sixpence," the shopkeeper answered, "I'll put one in a bag for you."

"No, thank you," replied Don handing him the money, "my small son 'shoplifted' one some months ago."

"Well, I'll be jiggered!" We left the man astounded.

One day I heard something in the larder. I lifted out the Corn Flakes to see the tell-tale signs that a mouse had been there.

"Quickly," I said to Don, "get Timmy, I'm sure there is a mouse."

Our well-fed cat showed total disinterest. Don said, "I'll get the little devil," and aimed his air pistol into the corner as I lifted up the Shredded Wheat box

99

tentatively. Bang, bang, the mouse was dead. Timmy then appeared and carried off the trophy proudly as if to say "Look what I've done, all my own work." An amusing drama.

Once Marion became seven years old, she was able to achieve her long held ambition to join the Brownies. Never was there a keener member of the Pack. She polished her belt, shoes and badge proudly before each meeting and worked hard to attain various badges, eventually becoming a "sixer". Caroline followed a couple of years behind her sister and was equally enthusiastic.

Two outings in particular when I accompanied the Pack, stand out in my memory.

One was a visit to the then new Festival Hall for a delightful performance of the ballet "The Nutcracker Suite", an excellent choice for a group of small girls.

The second outing was even more memorable. We went by coach to London to the vast and intriguing Science Museum. Each adult had charge of three Brownies. Mine were Marion, Caroline and Anne-Marie. Across the road from the Museum stood an equally impressive building, a favourite haunt of mine, the Victoria and Albert Museum. Provided we all met at the appointed time and place to leave in the afternoon, the groups were free to look at whatever they wished. We stayed in the Science Museum for an hour or so, then I took them to appreciate some of the superb ancient art treasures in the "V and A." We entered the foyer to see a large expectant crowd gathering.

"Whatever is happening?" I asked one of the bystanders.

"The King and Queen of Denmark are shortly coming on a special visit," the elderly gentleman replied.

"Ooo, can we see them too?" squealed Anne-Marie.

"Of *course* you can," he replied, "here, make room for these little poppets."

He pushed the three girls to the front of the crowd. Only a short wait and a car drew up. The King and Queen looked majestic, even without any crowns.

"Salute them, I whispered loudly to the girls. They did. Their reward was a dazzling smile from the King. They will remember that day all their lives. Later we went to visit the large Catholic church next to the Museum, The Brompton Oratory. To make the day perfect, a wedding had just taken place and the beautiful bride and retinue were awaiting the photographers. How excited the three little Brownies were when they met the others.

"We've had lots of adventures," said Anne-Marie, "we saw the King and Queen of Denmark. She didn't have a crown but wore a beautiful blue dress, *and* we saw a wedding." What an exciting day!

Very occasionally we took the children to visit a stately home or sometimes an art gallery. The big treat was being able to choose a postcard from the shop there, to keep. Marion's choice varied but she often chose a landscape. Caroline invariably chose a pretty lady. From a very early age, Oliver had a predilection for voluptuous nudes. We visited the National Gallery in London when he was still in his pushchair. His jaw fell open when he saw Rubens, huge "The Judgement of Paris". He screamed when we went to wheel him past it, so I put the brake on the pushchair and left him happily gawping as we walked around leisurely admiring the other paintings in the vast hall. By the time we emigrated he had quite a collection of naked ladies.

CHAPTER
NINETEEN

Honeythorne

The economy was healthy, a real consumer boom. We moved into a bigger house that gave us much more room.

We had extended the bungalow by adding another bedroom, but felt it was too small for our growing family. A new house was being built in a road off Brock Hill, Downham Road. It was almost completed and within our price range of £4,500. This detached chalet bungalow had the kitchen, living areas, bathroom and main bedroom on the ground floor. My hip was still quite painful after the operation I had when I was twenty-one to cure a congenital clicking hip. I feared the day would come when stairs would be a problem. Upstairs were two large bedrooms (for the children) and another lavatory and handbasin. The large eaves storeroom could have easily been converted to another room, in fact this was done by the next occupant. It was only a few minutes walk from "Wildthorne" so we frequently strolled there watching the completion of the building.

Our bungalow sold with no difficulty. We moved in December 1965. We heard that no road charges had been levied on this particular road when it had been recently made up. It was exempt because it was part of the original Roman road from London to Colchester. Once we dug up a very worn Roman coin, an exciting find. The large old shed at the bottom of the garden had originally been the habitation of the Londoners who owned the plot. They used it as a holiday home. Don planted honeysuckle and roses in the front garden and we named the house "Honeythorne".

It was now twenty years since the war ended. England had moved from austerity to a degree of affluence. Nearly twice as many people now owned a "Fridge" and a washing machine and many had a car. We still relied on my bike and public transport. Very slowly, supermarkets were starting to take the place of chain stores. There was a real consumer boom. No one saved for an item, they used hire purchase and had it *now*. My washing machine was the only item I paid for in this manner.

I have always loved markets, the bustle, the atmosphere and the bargains. As well as Wickford, and occasionally Chelmsford, sometimes I visited the large exciting Kingston market when I stayed with Valerie in Surrey. Dad had given Don and me beautiful initialled, filigree silver serviette rings for our first anniversary. Both Marion and Oliver had been given ones as babies, sterling silver with their names engraved, from different people. Caroline's serviette resided in a plastic ring.

One Friday, Valerie looked after the children and I indulged in the joy of an unfettered morning at the market. I saw a stall selling all sorts of knick-knacks. At the rear of the display I picked up a tarnished serviette ring that I quickly recognised as sterling silver by the lion on the hallmark.

"How much is this?" I asked the stallholder. "Oh dear, it already has initials engraved on it," I grumbled.

"Oh well, you can have it for 12/6," he said.

I could hardly believe it, it polished up beautifully and the three initials were Caroline's — C.R.D.

Wickford had no theatres or cinemas. During the twelve years I lived there I only went to the pictures three times. Once was to see Danny Kaye in "The Secret Life of Walter Mitty", and I took the children to Southend to see "The Sound of Music" and "Mary Poppins".

Good old "steam" radio was still popular in spite of the advent of television. Everyday at 1.45p.m. was the programme for small children, "Listen with Mother" and that is just what we did. We sang the songs together and listened to the story. Following this at two o'clock, was "Woman's Hour". If possible this was the time when the children had a rest or at least a quiet time with maybe a book or a puzzle. I tried to sit and enjoy this excellent broadcast, full of interesting features. Usually I caught up on any mending or ironing that needed to be done. (I remembered the recommendation by the orthopaedic surgeon who advised me to sit rather than stand and I used the adjustable "whizzy-round" stool.)

Each Tuesday we listened to "Hancock's Half Hour" with Tony Hancock, Sid James, Bill Kerr and Kenneth Williams, whose catch prase of "stop messing about" became immensely popular. We listened to "The Goons", "The Life of Bliss" with George Cole, and "The Navy Lark" with Ian Pertwee and Leslie Phillips's naïve instruction "left hand down a bit". Kenneth Horne in "Round the Horne" was such a favourite that I went to the Paris Theatre in London to watch the recording.

On Sunday evenings we were enthralled by Rupert Davies on the television in the "Maigret" series and "Dr Finlay's Casebook" with the handsome Bill Simpson. Some years later we watched "Upstairs, Downstairs" and "The Forsyte Saga" that continued for six months. I admired Kenneth More, Eric Porter and the ever youthful Susan Hampshire.

"Play School" each weekday had the children entranced with Humpty Dumpty, Jemima and Teddy. As they grew older they enjoyed "Jackanory" and "The Magic Roundabout" with Dougal, Zebedee and Florence. "Blue Peter" was a "must" as was Johnny Morris in his "Animal Magic" programmes from the zoo. We all watched the excellent "Railway Children" and "The Secret Garden". David Jason of Inspector Jack Frost fame must have made one of his first television appearances in "Mrs Black and the Cardboard Box Men".

"Softly, Softly" and "Z Cars", those exciting police dramas (and precursors of "The Bill"), were an important part of our lives. Each week I discussed the latest episode with my friends. What we really enjoyed were the many good comedy programmes that abounded in those days. Morecombe and Wise and Benny Hill were favourites of Don's. I have always loved the wit of Ronnie Barker in "The Two Ronnies" and the more gentle humour of James Bolam and Rodney Bewes in "The Likely Lads". Rolf Harris was just becoming popular with his flamboyant style of presentation and art and his fascinating "wobble board". The children loved him.

"Let's all sing that song we all sing," said Marion. "You know, we all sing Matilda!"

CHAPTER
TWENTY

The Clinic Job

A part time job with children all needing special care. Encourage their abilities and teach them how to share.

In January 1966 I saw an advertisement in the local paper for someone to run special Child Development sessions two mornings a week. Oliver was then eighteen months old but I hoped it would be a post where he could accompany me, and I was fortunate that my surmise was correct.

Various form filling dealt with, the interview loomed. There were six of us, all mothers looking for a convenient part time job. I was the lucky one chosen, as I had the necessary qualifications, the N.N.E.B. certificate (National Nursery Examination Board). How glad I was then that I had successfully completed the two-year course after leaving school.

This new experimental group mixed pre-schoolers with physical, mental or social handicaps. The last category mystified me, but I realised the need during the sessions. These were held on the premises of the Child Health Clinic in the town and run by the County

Council. We were well equipped and even had the luxury of "Dobbin", the large, popular rocking horse.

My assistant, Audrey, became a life long friend who had more than her fair share of tragedy. Her first husband had died when she was very young and expecting their baby. When Gillian was still small, she met Jack who loved children and they eventually married. Some years later to their delight she became pregnant and produced another little daughter, Jackie. Sadly, in those days no one was aware that German measles during pregnancy could cause birth defects. Jackie was born blind. She attended a special school in Wimbledon as a weekly boarder and was a very well adjusted girl. They were a delightful united family.

Jackie was a year or two older than Marion and we inherited many beautiful clothes that she outgrew and some very expensive toys. A large walking doll that we called "Jackie" was cherished as was the doll's cradle that is still a treasured family possession.

One day we invited Audrey and Jack to tea. Jackie had a school friend staying with her. Jenny had a heart defect and severe diabetes as well as being blind. At least, with the strict diet she needed to adhere to, she was unable to see the lavish spread I had produced. Audrey, being such a positive person, often said about Jackie, "Thank goodness her only defect is blindness.'

Caroline, then aged about five, was always very outspoken. I had explained to her that the girls were unable to see.

"You're blind, aren't you," she greeted Jackie.

I was horrified and tried to prevent further embarrassing remarks, but Audrey said, "Yes, that's right she is," and re-assured me saying, "She *is* blind and will have to learn that others will be aware of it."

The work at the Clinic was both interesting and challenging. We had a maximum of eight children as they needed constant supervision. One of the physically handicapped little girls had spina bifida. She reminded me of a mermaid, shuffling along using her elbows and dragging her useless legs. Both she and a similarly affected girl were incontinent and needed special care and attention.

We had two Down's Syndrome children. One dear little boy called Alec was the son of older parents. He loved music and our daily sessions with the percussion instruments and a rather temperamental gramophone delighted him. His parents and I attended the same church and each week persuaded Alec to go so that he could look for "Missee Day" as he called me. The poor little boy must have had many weeks disappointment after we emigrated. His mother said he searched each face hopefully. When the time came for us to pack and sell a lot of our furniture, they bought my treasured nursing rocking chair.

"What can I offer you to drink?" Don asked Alec's charming Polish father. He has always remembered his pertinent reply, "Anything except petrol!"

One profoundly deaf attractive, blonde, little girl, Christine, was with us for a short time before being assessed and sent to a special school. Marion was fascinated by this disability and always hoped one day to learn more about deafness and maybe specialise teaching hearing impaired children.

Another little boy, one of the "socially handicapped", was quite normal but both his parents were profoundly deaf. He, complete with striped woollen hat that he refused to remove, came to learn speech and help his baby brother to develop normally. At three and a half he communicated expertly with his mother using sign language. This was different from the "deaf and dumb" alphabet I had learned, but Mrs Briggs was able to understand and communicate slowly with me.

Sharon had recently moved to this country area after having spent the first four years of her life in a high-rise flat in the East End of London. Her only companion had been her mother. She joined us to learn how to play and socialise. It took her quite a while to adjust to both the environment and the other children. She stood by the wall, head down, sucking her thumb. Her one fascination was "Dobbin" the rocking horse and she waited patiently for her turn. Slowly, very slowly she became a happy member of the little group.

Ian, a delightful little boy, was unable to play at home as his brother Clive was autistic, limiting his activities considerably. This condition was a relatively new "discovery" and very distressing for his parents who had adopted both boys. Poor Clive had a clever mind locked inside his unco-operative brain and his behaviour was extremely erratic and totally unpredictable. He attended a special school. I have always kept in touch with the family and visited them a few years ago. Ian was then happily married with a small son doted on by his grandparents. Clive attended a Day Centre and had achieved a degree of normality. He actually made me a cup of tea to the great pride of his parents. His limited speech and actions were severely robotic. His father told me that Clive had been helping him dig the garden when he was called to the 'phone. When he returned some time later, Clive had continued following the original instructions and had carried on digging in the same spot, leaving an enormous hole. He told me he thought he might have dug his way to Australia if left much longer.

Eventually Audrey found a job with longer hours but we always remained close friends. Mrs Coward replaced her as my assistant and I worked at the Clinic happily for a couple of years until I too became more ambitious.

I was fortunate to be able to take Oliver with me. He was nearly two with a mop of curls that the other children could not resist pulling. Initially I was concerned about the school holidays as I only had a one month break during the summer. I found it presented no problem as Marion and Caroline came with me. I am sure their life-long love of small children and subsequent careers were nurtured by that experience as was their empathy with handicapped people.

Oliver accepted the other children with their various and varied disabilities and just became one of the group.

"When you have your overall on, you are not Mummy, you are Mrs Day."

The small pay packet I received each month was saved to pay for my first washing machine. Oliver still wore nappies when I started work and I had struggled along using the copper to boil our clothes. What pride I took in my new twin tub Hoover washing machine, completely paid for by my own efforts.

CHAPTER
TWENTY-ONE

Teachers College

To study was a challenge, I learned to use my brain
At Teachers College. Every day I travelled on the train.

Chatting to a friend about the future, I said, "How I regret now not having completed my final years at school and gone to Teachers College as originally planned. I have always loved children and it would have been an ideal career with a young family."

"It is not too late," she told me, "Brentwood College of Education is opening an extension at Southend especially for mature students, why don't you apply?"

I stored this knowledge in case I ever needed it. Oliver was not yet four and I had always enjoyed my children so much, I was loathe to have them cared for by someone else.

Marion's teacher at Blessed Anne Line School in Basildon invited me to spend a day in her classroom.

"You are welcome to bring Oliver too," she assured me. He happily busied himself with many diversions.

Mr Fox the headmaster had definite ideas about education. He had three children — "the three little foxes" — who reminded me of the A.A. Milne rhyme

Once upon a time there were three little foxes
Who didn't wear stockings, and they didn't wear
    sockses,
But they all had handkerchiefs to blow their
    noses,
And they kept their handkerchiefs in cardboard
    boxes.

In the "Infants" aged five to eight, there was no regimentation, formality or silence.

"Children should be encouraged to communicate when they are young," he told me, "with each other and with the teachers."

Shouting or yelling was never allowed but there was a constant hum of voices as they worked weighing containers of lentils, feathers and stones and noting comparisons. The little ones tried to count the aquarium fish. It was all very much a "hands on" experience. All the children loved school and learned many valuable practical skills.

Each Assembly Mr Fox played a piece of well known classical music such as Beethoven's Fifth Symphony.

"What does this music make you think about?" he asked. "Who knows the name of the composer who wrote the music?"

Lots of little hands shot up. This early introduction to music made a lasting impression on these young responsive minds.

Oliver and I shared the school lunch with the children, as did all the teachers. I had really enjoyed my day. It sowed the seed of what I would love to do one day. I have always lacked self-confidence and doubted my ability to be able to study or even be accepted for teacher training. No harm in applying, I thought and sent for the application forms. I agonised filling them in, fearing my lack of Higher School Certificate would exclude me.

We had a fairly straightforward exam. I remember having to write an essay on "Censorship". Then, to my surprise, I was asked to attend an interview. Eighteen of us, including three men, sat waiting apprehensively. We were called for individual interviews before a panel. I felt very scared. They asked me to read an article on meritocracy. I have always enjoyed reading aloud to the children and managed a reasonably creditable performance. I didn't stumble over some of the challenging words. *Then* they asked my opinion on meritocracy. I gasped, intent on getting my tongue around some of the complicated words, I had not absorbed the content of the article. Always be honest we had been taught at school.

"I'm afraid I don't even know what meritocracy means," I admitted.

My inquisitors looked meaningly at each other. Many other questions were asked including what would happen to Oliver until he was school age.

116

"That's all right, I have arranged with a neighbour to care for him," I assured them.

"What will you do if he or your daughters are ill?" they asked.

"If Don was at home, no problem, otherwise I would stay at home to look after them, there is no one else."

That's it, I thought, they won't want me now. I went home convinced I had failed.

To my great surprise, a few weeks later I received a letter of acceptance, giving me details of requirements for the start of my studies in September. I was truly shocked, but delighted.

Oliver, now aged four, was happy being looked after by a lady nearby who also had "baby Caroline". He enjoyed his time there and each day reported on the food.

"We had chocolate glue today." (Chocolate custard.)

One of his many questions on a similar subject after seeing on the television that someone was "in custody".

"Where is Custody?"

The hours at this outpost of Brentwood Teachers College were specifically adjusted for the mature students. The only problem could have been when children had a few days holiday at half term.

"You are welcome to bring them to the College," we were told, "after all, that is what education is about — children."

Marion and Caroline thoroughly enjoyed their few days joining me, especially watching their then lithe mother at P. E. classes.

We studied a wide variety of subjects including English, Religious Education, Nature Study which I loved, P.E. theory, Maths, Sociology, Psychology, History and Geography, Arts and Crafts (another favourite of mine) and Child Development. It was a very comprehensive course and quite a challenge to accomplish for someone who had not studied for over twenty years. I actually enjoyed the discipline of coping with the deadlines for the assignments and the research. No computers in those days but the College had an excellent reference library. A quotation that has long been a maxim of mine is "Failure will never overcome me if my determination to succeed is strong enough."

Studying to become a teacher was certainly a challenge with a home to run and children to care for and care about.

I looked forward to completing the course and finding a post in a local school. That would enable me to have an independent income and the hours meant I would not neglect my family — so important to me.

It was not to be.

CHAPTER
TWENTY-TWO

Plans

Squadron reunion, meeting George and Phil. Will we, won't we emigrate? I rather think we will.

My brother David, who had emigrated to New Zealand in 1948, was married to Dorothy and had three small sons. Occasionally I sent the boys each a postcard or even an "un-birthday" Ladybird book as a surprise gift. I know how exciting it is for a child to receive something addressed to them personally, by post. One of David's friends, Ron, came to England on business and visited us. We got a first hand report on David and his family and his home. We knew he had been a pilot in New Zealand for many years. Maybe this visit sowed the original seed that had us contemplating emigration.

Ron told us an amazing story. He had gone to Guildford in Surrey to visit my father who had lived in the same boarding house for many years. Ron left the station and started walking up the hill of the cobbled High Street of this large, old country town. On Sunday there were few people out for a stroll and he had no idea how to find Waterden Road. He saw an elderly gentleman wearing a suit and grey homburg hat.

"Could you by any chance direct me to Waterden Road?" asked Ron.

"Certainly," replied the gentleman, "I'm going there myself. I have just been having my daily walk."

Of all the people he could have stopped, it was Dad!

Don and I started discussing emigration seriously. He would like to go to Canada where he had many happy memories of his time there during the war when he did his R.A.F. training. (David had gone to Rhodesia for his pilot training.)

"Oh no," I begged, "let's go to New Zealand, and we would have someone there who would help us settle."

By now, Don was teaching Workshop Technology at Hackney Technical College, but felt ready for a change. He tried unsuccessfully for a post in Worthing, Sussex, a county we both loved. We had a few dear friends in Wickford, but no close family ties.

In 1967, just after my father's death, we seriously enquired about various emigration possibilities. Don was now in his mid-forties and too old to be considered for an assisted passage to Canada. It would have been impossible to pay our own fare anywhere as, although we lived fairly comfortably, we had no capital except in the house. The only "legacy" either of us has ever received was £50 from one of my aunts and the same from an uncle. New Zealand would only allow two children under their scheme, so we forgot the idea for a while.

I knew little about Australia. I visualised Sydney as a hot bustling city and the rest of the country as "outback". In April 1968 we tentatively sent for emigration information from Australia House.

During the war, Don had been a bomb aimer, flying Lancasters, and a member of 617 Squadron in the R.A.F. This squadron became famous as the Dambusters with good reason. This was made popular by Paul Brickhill's book and later the film starring Richard Todd. In those days Don spoke little of his wartime experiences and I was very surprised one day when he said, "I've just received a letter from my old squadron They are having a reunion at St Clements Church (dedicated to the R.A.F.) for the twenty-fifth anniversary of the Dambusters."

This was May 1968. I shall never forget the elation on Don's face when he returned from the reunion. He had not expected to see many of his old crew, as some were Australians.

"I was so surprised, there was my pilot Phil and wireless operator George from Australia. The R.A.F. flew in all the Australian and New Zealand crew members. Get out the 'red carpet'. I'm going out to buy some more whisky, we've got visitors tomorrow."

The two white haired, tall, bronzed Australians arrived, declining Don's offer of whisky. Phil said, "Oh, give us a cup of tea please."

George explained "We've been guests of the R.A.F. for a few days. It has been nothing but parties, booze and more booze."

They had both consumed more than their accustomed quantity of alcohol. When we mentioned that we were possibly contemplating emigration, Phil extolled the virtues of Perth in Western Australia, whilst George said the only place to live was Sydney.

At that time, Phil was a senior photographer on the "West Australian", Perth's daily newspaper. He was a very persuasive man. He sent us many editions of the Saturday paper which contained advertisements for employment and many tempting plans of bungalows.

"This sounds great, Don," I read aloud. "Three bedrooms, lounge, kitchen with dining area, bathroom, large garden with bricked-in area for a barbecue."

"What is a dineria?" asked Marion, mystified.

We started thinking seriously now and contacted Australia House for application forms to emigrate. We also visited Western Australia House in The Strand where they were most helpful and optimistic. They sent for us after a few months anxious waiting and we had our medical examinations. We wanted *nobody* to know of our enterprising plans until we were finally accepted. Marion had no problem keeping a secret, Oliver was too young to understand, but Caroline found it very difficult. She did manage to tell no one until we had our plans verified.

We heard on Don's forty-sixth birthday that we had been accepted as immigrants. The full cost for a family was £20 (or £10 for a single person, hence the title "ten pound Pom"). The condition was that we had to stay at least two years or repay the full fare. That was no problem as we went with the determination that we were going to "make a go" of it, come what may. I think two years is a very good stipulation as it gives one a chance to settle (or not) and experience all the seasons and benefits the new country has to offer. Some people were desperately homesick and couldn't cope with a new life away from their families and went back to England. Many of these returned to Australia later, paying their own fares once they had compared living standards, climate and all the other benefits "down under".

In those days international fares and even 'phone calls were prohibitively expensive. This made Australia seem even more remote. More than once I've been reminded of Aunt Stella's saying, "Distance isn't miles, it is l.s.d. (pounds, shillings and pence)" How true!

CHAPTER
TWENTY-THREE

Departure

Australia is beckoning, what to take or leave?
Making all our sad farewells, really made me grieve.

We applied to come by ship as I thought this would be a great experience and adventure for us all. In hindsight I am truly grateful that circumstances forced us to come by air. All my life I have suffered from severe travel sickness and I am sure that three and a half weeks on the sea would have been a nightmare for me, and Marion too.

Don needed to be in Perth in January to be interviewed for a teaching position so that he could start in the new school year. We had less than two months between acceptance and departure date.

Not one person knew of our emigration plans. Now we could tell people we were definitely going. I phoned Nickey.

"I'm sorry, we will not be able to come to Adam's eleventh birthday party."

"Oh, I'm sorry, why not?" she asked.

Then I dropped the "bombshell". "We'll be in Australia."

She was flabbergasted when I told her of our plans to go permanently.

I had never been out of England, not even to Wales or Scotland, so even I felt amazed at the enormity of our decision. Christmas was fast approaching so many of our friends were told of our plans in their Christmas card.

Then the panic started. So many decisions to be made. What to take? What to sell? What to give away? Don had been a successful and enthusiastic home-made wine maker for many years. He was storing a vintage collection. We gave bottles to close appreciative friends. The only furniture we decided to take was our Ercol dining suite and Don's Uncle Ernie's beautiful sapele mahogany bedroom furniture. No, it did not belong to him, he made it to our specifications for the new home we were about to leave. The built-in wardrobes, matching headboards and the two dressing tables he dismantled, naming each piece. We could not bear to part with them. He was such a very talented cabinet maker. The rest of our furniture sold by word of mouth, also most of the children's bigger toys, such as their climbing frame.

Sadly I handed in my notice at Teachers College. My biggest regret I had when emigrating was that I could not complete the course. I was really enjoying the challenge, the company and the promise of employment. Now I had no idea if I would even ever be employable in Australia.

A few weeks before departure, the airline B.O.A.C. contacted us with the good news that as emigrants, we were entitled to double baggage. This proved to be a great blessing as we were able to take our linen and some kitchen essentials.

"Choose your favourite toys," I told the children, "we can pack one suitcase with some and take them with us."

"Oh good, can we take Monopoly and some of our books?" asked Marion.

"No books," I told her "they will have to go by sea, they are too heavy."

We could not bear to part with our rapidly growing book collection. Then came the big problem. We, who never travelled other than a very rare holiday locally, had managed to scrounge five suitcases, now we needed another five, *and* at short notice.

"We can't afford to buy five suitcases for a one-off trip," said Don.

"I've got an idea," I suggested, "I'll phone the Citizens' Advice Bureau, they may be able to help." They came up with a good proposal.

"Try the W.V.S. (Women's Voluntary Service) at Chelmsford," they said. "They keep a store of donated suitcases for the prisoners when they are released from the jail."

Many of the cases were too big and unsuitable for them. We accepted them gratefully.

"How much do we owe you?" I asked.

"Nothing," the kind, buxom lady told me, "they were donated to us but if you would like to make a small donation that would be appreciated."

126

We gave a generous one, we were so grateful. Most of the cases survived the journey, *just*. My cousin Bernhard had given us two good quality solid cases, normally too heavy for air travel. One fitted inside the other and survived here over thirty years. They were used for storage or for various camps the children attended over the years.

"I'll need the 'big Bernhard' case this year," said Caroline.

The biggest problem that nearly caused cancellation of all our plans was "Dominoes". No, we were not addicted to the game, but we were to our dear little white spotted cat. It was not feasible to take her with us, as we couldn't possibly afford the high quarantine fees. She was too young and healthy to be "put to sleep". A well-loved family pet, we were really concerned about her.

"Let's ask our friends if anyone would like her." We tried, to no avail.

Don's cousin Rob and wife Beryl who lived in a town nearby, came for a final visit. We told them of our problem and with no hesitation Beryl said, "We'll take your little cat."

We were so relieved. Dominoes lived the rest of her life happily with their family.

All the good china we owned and other precious accumulated items were packed professionally. These would not be needed immediately, and were sent by sea with the furniture.

We were in a quandary what to do with our house. It was only four years old and we had made many improvements during those years, both inside and out. Very few people go house-hunting in England in January. Finally we decided to leave the deeds with the bank manager and it sold eventually in the spring.

I was so busy that last month that the realisation of the magnitude of our decision hadn't dawned. I really didn't know what to expect but just hoped the future would be bright for the children. I looked at the beautiful countryside now bare, the familiar places and faces and would try to combat the choking emotion knowing that I would never see them again. This is for ever I told myself, enjoy and appreciate all that is England, because you will never see it again. The finality of it all eventually caused tears, always private tears. I hate to cry publicly, the lavatory has always been my "weeping refuge".

During our final two weeks before departure, Don's niece Valerie and husband Bill kindly had the girls to stay with them in their small flat in Surrey. Oliver remained with us for the final packing, then we too stayed there, sleeping bags everywhere. Their daughter Nicola was just two and a little darling. They had problems with their television, the connection was unreliable. We were watching a "Carry On" film. Kenneth Williams carried a heavily laden tray. The picture wobbled so Bill gave the cabinet a thump and Kenneth Williams dropped the tray with an almighty crash! An amazing unforgettable moment.

We took the train for a final visit to London's West End. At Selfridges we bought a dozen polycarbonate glasses and a jug. They guaranteed they were unbreakable and had been demonstrated by a steam roller driving over one. I'm not particularly clumsy but glass items have always seemed to slip through my fingers so those were a wise investment. (Lightweight and easy to pack in our luggage.)

Bernhard and Vicki took us to the prestigious Mitre Hotel at Hampton Court for a sumptuous final lunch. I was so overcome with emotion I could hardly eat.

Vicki was on edge throughout the meal as she was anxious about their little Cairn terrier left in the car. Bernhard took Don aside.

"Remember, if you need financial help when you first arrive in Australia, don't hesitate to contact me."

Not only did he make this incredibly generous offer but so did brother-in-law Will. We were quite overcome by their kindness. All our capital was in the house and we emigrated with very little money. The rate of exchange then was about two dollars to the pound. We were always fiercely independent and would have had to be in desperate straits to have availed ourselves of these genuine and generous offers.

On our very last day we visited my dear school friend Maureen, husband Paddy and their three gorgeous children Louise, Paul and baby Catherine. They had very recently moved to nearby Stoke D'Abernon. We spent a wonderful nostalgic afternoon with them and I found saying goodbye shattering. I felt the same with Valerie and Bill, they had been so kind to us.

Bill took us to Heathrow where there was an unexpected delay. As the plane lifted off on my first ever flight, the butterflies in my tummy were not just of fear, but apprehension too. I looked down sadly on the patchwork of green fields convinced I would never see England again. Then, ever optimistic, I knew I was about to start a new exciting phase of my life.

CHAPTER
TWENTY-FOUR

Arrival in Australia

Feeling optimistic now we're on the 'plane.
This is an adventure to a new terrain.

What ambivalent feelings I had. Goodbye to England, hallo to Australia. Sadness, excitement, apprehension, optimism, I just did not know what to expect, but I would not be alone, my family were with me.

Poor Marion, she suffered badly from travel sickness *all* the way. Always inclined to diffidence she was probably also feeling very anxious about life in a new country. She was now aged ten, Caroline just eight and Oliver four and a half.

This was my first flight and fortunately the travel sickness that had always been the bane of my life was totally absent in the pressurised plane. I sat with Marion, Oliver and Caroline. Don sat across the aisle with an Italian girl.

"Careful, Mummy, you nearly sat on my 'twoducks', " complained Oliver as I returned to my seat after a necessary lavatory visit.

Each of my children aged three or four, had gone through a brief phase of having an imaginary companion. Marion used to talk to "Hallogonk". Caroline had a sexless creature for quite a while called "Pellep" and Oliver had his "twoducks". We had to walk carefully in case we trod on them and he would tell them stories at bedtime. We called them the "illegal immigrants"!

The B.O.A.C. plane stopped three times for refuelling on its way from London to Perth. Firstly at Tehran, we descended between towering mountains. The scenery was spectacular. This was the very first time I had been on foreign soil, and even at the airport, the exotic clothing and strange accents delighted and amazed me. Karachi struck us as hot and smelly even in the airport. At Singapore the damp blanket of humidity embraced us with its very distinctive odour.

"Oh, what *is* that smell?" asked Caroline. "I don't like it."

Hard to describe, it seemed a mixture of spices and drains, definitely oriental, but quite overpowering. We were glad to return to the plane after stretching our legs.

More food was served to us and Marion was sick once again, but now we knew we were soon approaching our destination. I had no idea then that I needed to exercise constantly and my ankles were swelling to huge proportions. They returned to normal after an anxious couple of days.

By the time we emigrated I was thirty-eight and Don forty-six, both beginning to get rather set in our ways. I had led a very insular life and never had any desire to travel, just yearning for the security of a home and some stability after the very unstable experiences of my childhood and adolescence. Still, I was open minded and flexible and prepared for the challenge of adapting to life in a very different environment. I am sure my expectations were realistic. Children enjoy new experiences and I guessed correctly that they would soon assimilate.

Here we were, touching down on the runway in Perth, the other side of the world. We had read in the excellent informative booklet "What Migrants Need To Know About Western Australia" that "W.A. is not paradise on earth, neither is it Britain with sunshine". We had left England ravaged by strikes, on a very wet, grey January day. Now the magnificent sunrise proclaimed the dawn not only of a new day but a new life for the Days.

PART TWO

CHAPTER
TWENTY-FIVE

First Weeks

Driving down to Meelup, how those "mozzies" bite. Settling back into our house. Washday a delight.

We arrived in Perth, Western Australia, on the 22nd of January 1969. The climate could not have been more of a contrast. Bright sunshine awaited us, as did Phil and May Martin and their children Deborah, Anne, Glenda and Owen. They had borrowed another car from Phil's cousin Olive Galliers, the Matron of the Armadale Kelmscott Memorial Hospital. What a marathon it must have been loading ten suitcases into the vehicles plus five bleary eyed immigrants.

Once all the paper work had been satisfactorily dealt with by the Immigration Officers at the Airport, we were driven straight to Phil's home in Kelmscott for breakfast. Fortunately Marion soon regained her equilibrium after her uncomfortable flight. Phil then drove us and our belongings to the house they had already rented for us in nearby Armadale.

We discovered that not only was the house fully furnished with even a television set and a small tricycle in the garage, but May had thoughtfully supplied a very essential item, lavatory paper. We had brought linen, cutlery, crockery and other necessary items with us in our bonus baggage allowance. The following day Phil arrived and said, "It's too bloody hot here for you Poms. I'm taking Don for his interview with the Education Department and when that is sorted out, we'll take you down south to Meelup where we spend our summer holidays."

I found it difficult for a long time to accept that in Australia one went south to get cool and north for the warmth. Similarly the positioning of one's house; one faced south to be cool. At least the sun still rose in the east and sank in the west.

Don was accepted to teach engineering maths and drawing to correspondence students from the country areas in this vast state. He would start early in February.

"Come on," said Phil, "I am taking the lot of you out to buy some thongs."

Whatever is a thong? I was mystified. So many things seemed strange. Even the roadside advertisement hoardings were something I had only seen on American films. We soon discovered that thongs were the rubber "flip-flops" that so many people were wearing in the hot Australian summer. To my surprise, many children and even some adults walked along the pavement (no, I had to learn to refer to it as a "footpath") barefoot. I wondered how they coped with the scorching surface, but realised they must have become acclimatised. The young boys were even playing "footie" (football) bare footed. I soon learned that "ie" was used as an abbreviation for numerous words. Mosquitoes were "mozzies", cockatoos "cockies", a "sickie" a day's sick leave, "brekkie" breakfast, "kindy" kindergarten, "postie" the postman and many, many others, but I was never sure why an egg was referred to as a "googie".

We had been in our house two days when Phil collected us for the four hours drive to Meelup. To my delight, I saw the one thing that epitomised Australia for me, a kookaburra. It sat at the roadside immobile with a snake in its mouth. It made me think of the familiar Girl Guide song

The kookaburra has no work, he has no work to
  do.
His job is in a tree to lurk and catch a snake or
  two,
And when he's cut that snake in half he sits up
  in a tree.
To ha, ha, ha, ha, ha, ha, ha, he, he, he, he,
  he, *he*.

I've never seen one with a snake since. Both at Meelup and back in Armadale, I frequently heard their uncanny laugh.

"Are we there yet?"

My children had never been for such a long car journey but we eventually arrived at Meelup. In those days, the beautiful bay was still totally unspoilt. A few cars and a sprinkling of tents and caravans nestled under the shade of the large, fragrant, peppermint trees right on the beach. A small wooden hut in the bush housed the primitive lavatory. The Martins camped there each summer with two large tents. A caravan awaited our family.

Never before, apart from my brief Girl Guide camping experience, had we camped or caravanned. Not only were we in a strange country, but thrust into an unfamiliar life-style too. We managed. The children, now aged ten, eight and four, enjoyed the sandy beach. Marion and I suffered badly with sunburn, sunstroke and those wretched mozzies. The word had spread in the mozzie kingdom that there was a family of Poms with nice tender skin and they attacked us voraciously. We smothered ourselves with insect repellent to little avail. I thought of the pertinent rhyme by Ogden Nash

One bliss for which there is no match
Is when you itch to up and scratch —

Phil and May kindly took us out and about but I found the whole new experience too bewildering and unsettling. I just felt that I would like to settle in our house and concentrate on *adjusting*.

I had read many books on Western Australia prior to our departure and was aware of the dangers of spiders and snakes. Mesmerised in horror I gaped at the huge huntsman spider above me in the Martin's tent.

"It's all right," they said casually, "it eats the flies and mozzies." Ugh!

The walk to the smelly little lavatory petrified me. I was convinced that a snake or spider would attack me.

140

I have never been so constipated in my life! Actually, Western Australia's only dangerous spider, the small "red back" could possibly have been lurking under the seat, a favourite hide-away of theirs. They have a poisonous bite but are not aggressive.

Many years had passed since our minicar accident but I still felt nervous in a car. When Phil ate a sandwich with only one hand on the wheel, I was sure we were about to crash. Always a very poor car or coach traveller, I had to fight progressive nausea both ways on that long trip.

We returned to Armadale to settle into the house a week before school was due to start. The local Catholic primary school, St Francis Xavier's, to my surprise involved fees. Catholic education in England had been free. Still, we reckoned we could manage as Don would be teaching by then. Our capital was still in our unsold house. We managed to live with all the necessities but strictly no extras. The girls' uniforms now consisted of a green check dress with a circular skirt. I borrowed a couple until the arrival of my sewing machine. No talented dressmaker, I then tackled the rather daunting design. Their nearly new, scarlet pullovers I dyed the required navy blue. To do this, I first had to dye them green to neutralise the red, then re-dye in navy blue — reasonably successful.

Amazingly, both Marion and Caroline settled into their new school. The rigid system run by strict nuns and sitting at desks in pairs could not have been more of a contrast to the relaxed atmosphere at "Blessed

141

Anne Line School". Children seem able to adjust and conform easily.

Meanwhile, Oliver and I sweltered in the intolerable heat, no air conditioners then, my first experience of "century" heat (100°F).

"Mummy, come and play with me."

Oliver's plaintive cry had us playing Snakes and Ladders or "little cars". He missed his friends and his sisters. I would have felt desperately lonely without his company. I think those first few months were the only time in my life that I have experienced boredom.

Our goods were still on their way so I did not even have the consolation of familiar possessions. Without a vehicle, Oliver and I trudged along the side of the unfenced railway to the shops, quite a distance.

"What are those funny hard black things?" he asked in the greengrocers.

Neither Oliver nor I had ever seen a passion fruit. The bitter cumquats, loquats, delicious mangoes, avocadoes and, later, chinese gooseberries (kiwi fruit) were all new tastes. We quickly learned to examine stone fruit for the insidious little maggots of the fruit fly.

So many things were new. Pushchairs hung on hooks behind the buses, "roo" bars on the front of the cars, also sunshields. No letter box in our front door, but on a post by the footpath where the milk was left too. The request "bring a plate" when invited out, did not mislead me. Unlike many new migrants, I did not arrive with an empty plate. Some of the idioms I found different but expressive, such as a "full bottle" for a know-all and "sticky beak" for nosey parker. I had to learn new

142

names for clothing too. A vest was now a singlet, bathing costume — bathers, anorak a parka, gym shoes — sneakers. Even the ice-creams confused me. At Meelup Phil said, "Right, let's go to the shop and you can all have a drumstick."

Expecting a chicken leg, I was surprised and delighted with the ice-cream in a crispy cone. Yet another word, not cornet, cone.

I discovered that living a suburban life was not unlike what we had left. Shop and bank hours were the same, our diet too. We enjoyed many of the familiar television programmes though were also aware of a strong American influence. The pattern of our day was similar. One thing that was very different was the ease with which the clothes dried on washing day. The uncertain English climate had always caused big problems. No clothes lines here but an efficient rotary hoist.

The house we rented had a wood stove in the separate laundry to heat the water. We found it hard to believe that the fuel was free in the bush. Phil initially accompanied us in our forays, with his chainsaw. We also had a wood stove to heat the sitting room. We did not mourn the hefty English heating bills.

We had barely been in the house a month and were just settling in when to our alarm the owners decided to sell it. Had we already sold our house in England, we could have bought it for just over $11,000. It was fine for a temporary rental house but not what we would have wanted permanently. To our great relief, it was bought as an investment. We were able to continue renting there, but it *did* cause a degree of consternation at the time.

Perth is Australia's sunniest city and also the windiest. During the winter it rains heavily in short heavy falls, a similar annual average to England. The days were not unlike an English summer. Apart from a few exceptionally hot days, the climate we found to be idyllic.

CHAPTER
TWENTY-SIX

Settling In

Feeling rather homesick. Buying wholesale meat.
Girls were happy at their school, mothers I could greet.

A month or so after our arrival I heard a squeaking sound outside. It was not the trill of a magpie or the squawk of a parrot. I could now recognise those sounds.

"Come on, Oliver," I said, plucking up my courage, "let's see what strange creature is outside."

There, at the foot of the steps sat a tiny tabby kitten. "Tiger Tim" as we named him, proved to be a great diversion and delight to all the family. We had no idea how he appeared there but suspect he was dumped by a neighbour. We were missing Dominoes who we heard had settled happily. Tiger Tim even came with us when we went to the bush, always coming when he was called.

I was unprepared for the homesickness and loneliness. Each day I awaited the postman hopefully, spending a lot of time writing "home".

Slowly the months passed and I acclimatised to my new environment. Then, in April two propitious events occurred. Firstly, our goods arrived from England. What an ordeal to try to fit everything into our already furnished house. Fortunately the garage held quite a few boxes. I have always been acquisitive and possessions have meant a lot to me, probably too much. It was a great consolation to have my own belongings again.

A letter arrived from England.

"The house has sold at last," Don told me. "Now we can really start looking for blocks of land."

We liked Armadale, the girls were settled at school, so we looked locally. We found a quarter acre block we liked in an established area on a rather steep incline, with wonderful views to the coast. The sunsets were magic. Facing directly west was a big mistake with the heat but we later successfully applied reflective window treatment. The position was excellent as it was only a short walk to the station for Don and also to the school and church and not too far to the shops. These factors were vital as we had no car.

"Hop in my car, Don," Phil said, "I'm going to give you a driving lesson."

It didn't take Don long to learn and obtain his licence. We bought a Holden FJ car which we used until Phil sold us his station wagon a year or so later. Petrol was about forty cents a gallon. They often called to see us and always departed with "See you later."

I waited and waited, cups and saucers ready. I felt most disconcerted that there was no return visit. It took me a long time to realise the phrase was the English equivalent of "goodbye".

146

May knew that Oliver and I were trapped in the house for most of the time and occasionally collected us for an outing. Thinking she was giving me an enjoyable diversion, she took us to an abattoir near Fremantle to buy meat wholesale. I really dreaded those days but was far too intimidated to refuse. Seeing all the carcases hanging up and the animals' macabre heads on shelves made me shudder. I felt totally repulsed and had to fight nausea at each visit. I think my progressive disinclination for red meat stems from those days.

Admittedly, the meat was excellent and cheap, four dollars for eight pounds of steak. Don bought our meat weekly and told me what I was to cook each day.

Not long after we arrived I needed to visit the doctor. In the crowded waiting room I sat next to an elderly man. He told me he worked on a farm and had come to have *wheat* removed from the back of his hands.

"Wheat?" I said, "You mean wheat that you harvest?"

"Yes," he answered, "the seeds get under me skin an' I don't know they're there 'till they start sprouting."

I was horrified, what sort of country had I come to? Never since have I come across this phenomenon.

Two kind Irish ladies Brid and Rita collected me one evening and took me to a Majellan meeting. I had no idea what the word Majellan signified. I knew of the explorer Ferdinand Magellan and was mystified how he was connected to the Catholic church. I found it to be a "laid-back" women's fellowship group founded in Perth only ten years previously. I was fairly knowledgeable with my hagiography but had never heard of the Patron Saint of Mothers, St Gerard Majella. No pressures were involved, no fees, no expectations. Sometimes we had a relevant speaker, sometimes we just shared experiences. In this huge country the motto used to be "Populate or perish". Many of these ladies certainly insured against extinction. The size of some of their families amazed me. Many of my friends there had eight or nine children and one delightful lady had recently produced her tenth. They all seemed to cope.

Most had children at the school and now I was able to greet quite a few by name. This really helped me combat the feelings of isolation. I tentatively joined the tuckshop roster helping sell pies, pasties, and homemade cakes that we baked ourselves.

"Can you help us with the Lamington Drive?"

Now I was really perplexed. I couldn't drive and where was Lamington? I was soon enlightened. Lamingtons were the delicious cube-shaped cakes I had already enjoyed. Huge slabs of sponge cakes were cut up, dipped in chocolate icing, then immersed in coconut. Finally they were boxed and sold as a fund raiser.

That first July we watched our televisions with the rest of the world, enthralled at the unbelievable spectacle of men actually walking on the moon, an unforgettable day.

The wonders of technology have always astonished me. How can a huge plane become airborne? How can a minute integrated circuit operate a watch? As for the computer functioning, my mind boggles. How I wish I could have learned science at school. Biology and Botany both fascinate me. I could hardly believe the proliferation of brightly coloured parrots and cockatoos. We even had the rare privilege of a pair of blue wrens nesting in our climbing rose. The window treatment being reflective, the brilliant blue male could see a rival and bashed his beak repeatedly against the glass in territorial rage. Daisy our cat sat less than an inch away on the window sill, but invisible, chattering with fury in her frustration. Quite a pantomime!

My birthday in October in England was always spectacular with the variegated colours of autumn. Now it is in the spring, equally lovely but different. Everything seems to blossom, no wonder Western Australia is called the Wildflower State. It is strictly forbidden to pick any of the wildflowers, so it took me a long time to get to know any of them. As I walked along the path by the side of the railway to the shops I counted over twenty different species. I could identify the beautiful blue leschenaultia, the various yellow wattles and the scarlet bottlebrush. I learned to say "Anigosanthos manglesii", a very impressive name for our State flower, the unusually shaped kangaroo paw. The uninspiring looking boronia has a wonderful perfume as do many of the eucalypts, peppermint and lemon-scented too.

I missed my familiar horse chestnut trees, ancient oaks and elms, and particularly the hedgerows. No hedges here, just wire fencing around the paddocks. (Yes, I remembered not to say "fields".)

In Australia some trees have most unusual names such as the Snottygobble, Lilly Pilly and Bottlebrush. I grew to love the variety of trees from the majestic Moreton Bay fig trees to the aromatic native frangipani and of course the huge variety of eucalypts.

CHAPTER
TWENTY-SEVEN

New Home
"Down Under"

Our house has sold in England, we can build a new one here, Don and I are both employed, a memorable year.

Once we had bought the block of land, we had to decide on a builder. They proliferated in those days. Our only method of discriminating between them was to view the workmanship of the many houses being erected locally. Eventually we chose a small building company, long since defunct. They gave us the personal attention we required. I discovered I was referred to as "the lavatory lady" as when discussing plans I insisted on two lavatories. This word was obviously rarely used in Australia. Our final decision was a modification of one of their plans. It consisted of three bedrooms, sitting/dining room, large kitchen/diner and a *huge* laundry with a second lavatory and shower. This room extended to a long roofed-in area that we subsequently converted to a fourth bedroom. A few years later we also added a large family room, a real boon. This was where the jigsaw puzzles could be left unfinished, or a quiet place for crafts, or entertaining the children's friends without disturbing Don.

There were so many choices to be made. The colour of the bricks, roof colour, paint, tiles, bathroom fittings and many other items. It certainly kept me occupied in the idle months of my first winter.

Caroline had always been a very enthusiastic and competent Lego builder. We invested in a large wooden box of those versatile plastic blocks when the children were very young. She organised us and together we built the house in Lego, to show the builder just what we wanted. The windows were not the correct size but otherwise it was to scale. Oliver enjoyed walking his little fingers from room to room eventually saying delightedly, "and this will be *my* bedroom."

We moved in on Boxing Day, just eleven months after arriving in Perth, settled happily now in our own home.

Meanwhile the girls were enjoying the universality of the Guide movement and joined the local Brownies. The names of the "Sixes" were different but the system was the same. Marion, soon ready to progress to Guides, was the last Brownie in Armadale to enjoy the charming ceremony, now sadly obsolete, of "flying up". It was made an extra special occasion complete with cake and the Commissioner in attendance.

That first November I was initiated in the delights of garage sales. An old house nearby, whose elderly occupant had died, had most of the contents for sale.

152

Don bought some useful garden tools. I enjoyed fossicking for "treasures" in the many old suitcases.

"Oh my goodness, whatever is this?"

I backed away. No, it was not one of the many cockroaches I was encountering, ugh, but a number of sets of false teeth grinning up at me. Life is full of surprises! It didn't deter me. I have always liked pre-loved items. I prefer the mellow patina of old jewellery to shiny new gold.

Still mourning the loss of my curtailed career in teaching, I enquired about continuing locally. This was my biggest regret when we immigrated. I was made aware that there was nothing available that did not require a lot of travelling. Not only did I have no car but I couldn't drive. Armadale is about twenty miles south of Perth and the outermost suburb of the Metropolitan area. Beyond, it is classed "country". Child Care Centres that I was admirably qualified for did not exist then. The working wife in Australia, unlike England, was a fairly new phenomenon. My only other avenue was the Pre-School Board. I 'phoned them to be told curtly, "No, we only employ qualified Kindergarten teachers."

My disappointment acute, I persisted and offered my services as an aide. I was given a couple of weeks' relief work in the winter.

I knew nothing of the system here. I learned that the Pre-Schools were run by a committee of parents with government subsidies. They charged about two dollars a week and the few around had long waiting lists. Children started school in February the year they turned six, older than in England, just the one intake a year. I tried to enrol Oliver at Armadale Pre-School for the third term but there was no vacancy. Mrs Clarke was retiring and hoped to leave before the end of term.

"Vood you come and teach ze last veeks?" she asked me in her thick Dutch accent. The Pre-School Board approved and with some trepidation I managed to run the kindergarten for the last weeks of term. The children seemed so *big*, some nearly six years old. A big advantage of this job was that Oliver could accompany me. Fortunately I had the support of Nancy. She was the aide, an attractive, blonde lady. Not only was she hard-working and efficient, but she knew the children. It was a real challenge as it involved end of year concerts and parties and a lot of responsibility suddenly thrust upon me. I coped. Obviously I must have been satisfactory as to my delight, the Pre-School Board offered me permanent employment as a trained aide. There were two groups, each comprised of thirty-six five-year-olds. There would be a teacher in charge who coped with all the administration, an untrained (but experienced) aide Nancy, who did jobs such as cleaning the paint pots, preparing the play-dough, and me. I was "pig-in-the-middle" and worked happily with both my colleagues.

Don spent the first term of the year with the Education Department marking correspondence students' papers. He was not happy there and looked for more stimulating employment. He saw an advertisement for a Supervising Technician at the then embryo Western Australian Institute of Technology, always referred to by its acronym W.A.I.T. He applied for the post in the Mechanical Engineering Department but that had already been filled. He was offered a similar position in the Civil Engineering Department which he accepted. Their premises were then in central Perth in St George's Terrace prior to moving to the huge new campus being built at Bentley. Later it became Curtin University of Technology, named after John Curtin, a West Australian who became Prime Minister of Australia during World War II. Don was promoted to Laboratory Manager after a few years and remained there happily until his retirement in 1987.

What an eventful year that was. We migrated, sold our house in England and had a new one built here. Don had a permanent job and so now did I. The children were all thriving and enjoying their new life. I had now settled and was fast making new friends. Life was good.

CHAPTER
TWENTY-EIGHT

Differences

Words pronounced a different way, learning metrication. Don in shorts and knee high socks. Quite a revelation!

Living in Australia was almost like moving to another world with a totally different culture. In England "Mummy and Daddy" were the common form of address for parents. (Maybe *not* so "common" as Prince Charles refers to the Queen as Mummy!) Here, once one starts school, it is Mum and Dad. I found more and more words and phrases that were dissimilar, especially as I tend to be pedantic.

H, aitch, was often pronounced haitch; burglar, burgular; cutlery, cutelry; film, filum; maroon, maroan; One went to a "triffic letcher". Shown and grown developed an extra syllable — showen and growen. Our own family provided its own mispronunciations. One child always read the word motif as mofit; buttocks as buttnocks (a lovely word), and another enjoyed the Dr Doolittle books by "Huge" Lofting. We abbreviated polyester and cotton to "potton".

Euphemisms were plentiful. One didn't die, one expired or passed away; naked was in the altogether; lavatory a convenience, comfort stop or toilet; fart, pass wind; a lie a fabrication; and many, many more. Sentences might end with the word "but" or "ya know". It was the tautology that has always amused me — "kills flies dead", "a new innovation", "reiterate again", and "also too". I bought an article that declared it was "almost semi-permanent!"

To greet someone it could be "g' day" or "what do you know" and the farewell "hoo-roo" or "'ave a good day". Very different from the conventional hallo and goodbye I knew. The verbosity, particularly of politicians, was and still is astonishing. "Now" could be "in this day and age" or "at this point of time", "yes" "you're not wrong". I found West Australians had very little "Aussie" accent, just sometimes an upward inflection of the voice at the end of a sentence, as if asking a question.

Getting used to the monetary system after sterling was quite easy. Australia had become decimalised about three years prior to our arrival and dollars and cents were straightforward. Gradually metrication changed our way of thinking. No longer was 100°C the "century". Distance had changed, instead of living 18 miles south of Perth, we were now 30 kms. It took a long time to adjust to the new method but slowly, very slowly, one begins to think metric. I remember being told that when you are learning a new language, once you begin to dream in that language you have really mastered it.

When we first arrived the fashion was long hair for young men and flares. The older ones wore smart walk shorts and long socks. I thought they looked like overgrown boy scouts and was amazed to see businessmen in the city dressed in them. Don, who had always been very conventional with a white shirt and tie, took happily to shorts and gradually even wore coloured shirts. Mini skirts were the young women's fashion, definitely not for me.

A popular hobby then was macramé. That had come and gone in England but here wall hangings, pot plant holders and macramé classes were very popular. I enjoyed learning my knots at Girl Guides, but this had no appeal for me at all.

A few years after our arrival we watched our black and white television on Christmas Day in 1974. We were horrified to see the devastation caused by Cyclone Tracy that demolished Darwin. A few months prior to our arrival, Meckering (a township 150 kms north east of Perth) had been badly damaged by a severe earthquake. We knew Australia suffered such catastrophes but felt insulated in Perth. The worst we saw was a willy willy. This is an amazing sight, a miniature whirlwind. I saw one once a few metres away only about a metre in diameter. Leaves gyrated frenziedly for a minute or two and then it was over.

1975 was International Women's Year. Women were now being noticed and being accepted and appreciated for their contributions to the family, the business world and society. Equal pay for equal work was slowly being achieved many years after British women had campaigned successfully. Everything seemed that bit slower in Perth but we found that part of the attraction. Many of the other Australian cities were hardly aware of our existence; the distance is so great. We tend to refer to them as "over East". Perth is the most isolated city in the world.

In comparison with the sunny summers the winter evenings could be quite chilly. Some form of heating was necessary although we never needed an overcoat or gloves.

Our new home had an efficient, labour saving, gas heater in the sitting room and another in the family room. Many people had wood fires or oil heaters. Our house made of conventional cavity brick construction, retained the heat, but also unfortunately the summer heat. Many older houses were "fibro". This was made from asbestos cement sheeting which was much cooler in the summer. This method of construction was discontinued in the late 1970s when the dangers from asbestos dust were acknowledged. Sad cases of asbestosis and mesothelioma were diagnosed up to twenty years later from those who had lived and worked in the mining town of Wittenoom.

One of these was my dear friend Ruth's husband who died in 1988. A few years earlier he had been a local hero, as he had rescued his baby grandson from their burning home. This tragedy occurred while the family was enjoying a barbecue on the patio. The wooden house was suddenly engulfed in flames. Brian rushed in and managed to rescue little Nathan. The family, who still had five of their eight children living at home, lost everything. They had no insurance. That evening many of their friends gathered to see what they could do to help the immediate problems. Some lent caravans for them to sleep in temporarily. Ruth and Brian had a large orchard. The packing shed became their living area for some months. The local community all helped with labour and materials to eventually build a substantial brick home.

The evening of the crisis I knew Ruth literally only had what she stood up in. She had envied a particular dress of mine so I gave it to her as a small contribution. The following day she was interviewed on television wearing it.

"Mum, Mum," called my excited daughter. "Come and look, your dress is on television!"

We enjoyed the more casual and relaxed lifestyle and knew we would never want to return to live in England. A few years later we were proud to take Australian citizenship. Hopefully if we were called "pommie bastards" it was in affectionate terms.

CHAPTER
TWENTY-NINE

David's Visit and Ours to New Zealand

David so resembled Dad, I had to look again. New Zealand I found magical, we went by train and plane.

Originally we were a happy family, mother, father, two much older brothers, Jack and David, and me. My mother suffered declining health for some years and died the year after Jack's tragic death, when I was eleven. Dad lived a quiet life in his boarding house in Guildford and David, my beloved brother, had emigrated to New Zealand.

Actually, due to various circumstances, we had spent very little of our childhood together. He visited me at boarding school when he could and wrote regular letters. Although six and a half years my senior, we were always very close. After Dad's death David was my only near relative. He actually took his family with him for their first visit to England in 1969. He had left in 1948. We missed them by a few months. I felt so disappointed and frustrated. Still, he promised it would not be long before they visited us and the great day arrived the following August.

"What is Uncle David like?" The children were as excited as I was.

"Well, he has blue eyes, wavy hair and is very handsome," I replied.

Twenty-two years had passed since I saw him last; I had never met his wife Dorothy, or Derek and Michael. Our whole family went to the airport to meet them. David, being a pilot, had concession fares but was on "stand-by". We knew his proposed flight number and all sat on a bench watching the arrivals. They were coming via Melbourne.

"Hallo, Eve."

I felt a tap on my shoulder and spun around to see Dad smiling at me. I blanched, was I seeing a ghost?

"It's O.K.," David said reassuringly, "it *is* me, we managed to get on an earlier flight from Melbourne." He gave me a warm hug.

He looked remarkably like Dad with the identical hairstyle — quite bald! After my initial shock I realised that twenty-two years was a long time and we had all grown older. Their eldest son Jack had visited us briefly the previous year en route to England. Dorothy and the two younger boys, Derek and Michael, aged about fourteen and sixteen, accompanied David.

They spent a happy week with us and David and I tried to catch up on our years apart. They showed us slides of their world trip that had included England.

"Oh, look, look," shrieked an excited Caroline, "there's Uncle Harry."

Not only had they photographed him but had also audiotaped him reminiscing. His distinctive gravelly voice is a nostalgic treasure.

"Where are we going today?" the boys asked us eagerly.

We had already visited beautiful Kings Park on Mount Eliza in the city. This large area, of natural bush has magnificent views of the area including the tranquil Swan River.

"We're going to Serpentine Falls, not too far away," we told them.

Being winter, everything was green and the waterfall copious. We were bitten by mosquitoes and the boys delighted in teasing their cousins. Their parents took them to Perth on the train another day, a huge excitement. This family had been around the world on many planes. They had hired cars in different countries but our suburban train was the first train they had ever been on. We visited Fremantle and talked and talked and talked. Oh! It was wonderful to be with my adored brother.

"Goodbye," said David at the airport as they departed, "and don't leave it too long until you come and stay with us, we'd love to show you New Zealand."

I felt so dejected as they left. Their visit inspired me to save my wages to enable us to do just that. The following year in the summer school holidays the whole family headed to Auckland for a month.

"The flights are very expensive," I told Don. "How would you feel if I found out about travelling to Sydney by the new train, the 'Indian Pacific'?"

This added another week to the holidays as it took three days to travel from Perth by the Indian Ocean to Sydney by the Pacific Ocean, hence the name of the train. I discovered the fares were actually cheaper then than flying and all the meals were included. The cabins we slept in were cleverly designed for two people and even had a handbasin. The economic use of the space amazed me.

The lounge car's huge picture windows gave us a panoramic view of the scenery. It seemed an eternity passing through the Nullabor Plain, aptly titled, as there are no trees. The desert of inland Australia just produces scrub.

"Oh Mummy, look, a kangaroo — and another."

At dusk it was a big thrill to see them hopping parallel to the train. The original train transversing the continent was referred to as the "Tea and Sugar" train. It stopped, as it still does now, at the very remote settlements to bring their necessary provisions. Three or four houses for the railway maintenance crews was all there was for hundreds of miles. There used to be one teacher schools to cater for the few children in these very isolated locations. The scenery changed after we reached Port Augusta in South Australia. Now it was less harsh and much more interesting and varied. Prior to arriving at Sydney we had the thrill of crossing the sensational Blue Mountains.

The trip was never boring as we were all omnivorous readers, and had also taken Scrabble and a pack of cards with us. The food was varied, plentiful and excellent. We had great admiration for the waiters in the

Dining Car who carried their laden trays so efficiently, lurching in all directions as the train swung around a bend. It was a very exciting and educational trip for us all.

At Sydney, we collected our luggage and took a taxi to the Airport. We looked in the Duty Free shop and, with not long to wait, were all aboard the plane for Auckland, and there were David and family waiting to greet us.

Their beautiful large home had lawns that swept down to Lake Pupuke. Only a short stroll across the road and we were on Takapuna beach, what a beautiful position. We arrived on December 23 and I was surprised and very disconcerted when Oliver, then aged seven, whispered urgently, "Mum, do you think Father Christmas will know I am in New Zealand?"

Panic! We hurried to the local chain store and bought a few appealing, disposable items. Father Christmas always filled one of Don's socks with "goodies". This was placed at the foot of each bed. Father Christmas was then easily able to replace the empty one with a full one. Their Christmas gifts were from *us*, not Father Christmas.

One item in Oliver's stocking was a false nose and glasses which David enjoyed playing with too!

They took us on lots of outings. One day we went to the hot springs at Waiwera where, as well as bathing in these therapeutic pools, we were fascinated to walk on the beach and find warm patches where the water rose in hot bubbles. They took us to the Zoo and Transport Museum where we were actually able to clamber on to

165

a real Lancaster aircraft, the type Don flew in during the war. In the centre of Auckland we visited the Domain with its magnificent gardens, hot houses and fernery. Oliver always said the great love affair of his life stems from his New Zealand visit, his passionate love of ferns. It was the peak of the strawberry season so one day we all went strawberry picking. We were enjoying gobbling these luscious ripe fruits when Oliver who had his basket nearly full, innocently said "Oh, are we allowed to *eat* them too?"

He had virtuously been resisting the temptation.

David borrowed a car for us and after a week or so at Takapuna, our dentist from England, who had now returned to Hamilton, came to meet us and we followed him to his home. How excited we all were to see each other again. Joy and George not only had Anita and Linda but now also delightful blonde three-year old Glen. He loved running away and had even managed to scale the high fence in their garden. They took us to the thermal region not far away from Hamilton and we visited the famous Maori settlement at Rotorua. I kept tight hold of Glen's hand as we were terrified he would fall into an unfenced, menacing, gurgling mud pool.

"That's a horrible smell, I don't like it."

Oliver's sensitive nose was assailed by the pungent smell of sulphur emitting from the pools.

None of us liked it, but just as I had heard, after a while one is not so aware of it. The actual sight of the bubbling, swirling mud mesmerised and fascinated me. We were most impressed by the displays of Maori

166

culture. Another day George said "We must take you to Waitomo caves."

We all donned our raincoats and waited in the queue for our tickets. I believe New Zealand averages about 180 days rain a year, no wonder the place looked so green and lush.

"Hallo, Joy, it *is* Joy isn't it?"

The voice behind us made me spin around and there to my surprise was a face I knew, but couldn't quite place. Mary and Graham had lived in Chelmsford in England not far from us, he like George was a dentist. I had seen Mary at the parties held by Joy. What a small world, that we should be visiting the caves at the identical time. They were on a cruise and had one day only in Auckland. They had hired a taxi to take them to see some of the outstanding (if distant) sights.

Waitomo Caves were certainly spectacular with very impressive stalactite formations and amazing acoustics. Then we boarded a boat and were warned to be absolutely silent. We glided eerily into the inky, almost tangible blackness — not a sound — and there they were, millions and millions of glowworms, an unforgettable sight. The slightest noise and their lights are gone.

Joy and George took us to Lake Taupo, a huge lake caused by the biggest volcanic eruption ever known. It is now full of trout and very popular with fishermen. We returned via Cambridge, a charming town very reminiscent of England, in fact I felt that New Zealand had a far more English atmosphere than Australia.

The holiday had been a delight. I had seen my dear brother and his family and renewed the friendship with the warm hospitality of Joy and George. We also had the opportunity to see some of the beautiful diverse countryside. We had left crisp, brown paddocks in the Australian summer and in New Zealand we revelled in the familiar bright, green grass. No wonder the milk chocolate even tastes different with the cows' lush pasture. We returned to David's home for a short while.

Three weeks had sped by and soon we were on the plane returning to Sydney for a few days. Here we were guests of George, Don's wireless operator from 617 Squadron, and his wife Daphne. They welcomed us to their home and somehow managed to squash us all in. John and Neil, their sons, were of a similar age to our girls. As soon as they saw the familiar box, Marion said joyfully "You've got Monopoly!"

The four of them happily immersed themselves in this addictive game. The following day George announced "Come on all of you, I'm taking you out to see the sights. We'll drive around and look at the Opera House, the Harbour Bridge and have a picnic at Cook's Landing."

"I'm not going," said Marion defiantly, "I want to keep playing Monopoly."

"Yes, you are," I assured her. "You'll never get this opportunity again."

"You can take me if you like but I don't *want* to see them, I'll close my eyes."

She was so strong willed that she probably did.

168

Don and I enjoyed our interesting and informative though brief time with them, then it was all back on to the Indian Pacific train for the return journey to Perth. We had a stop at Broken Hill. I remember the opera singer whom we had thrilled to in England in "The Merry Widow". June Bronhill. She took her name from this, her home town, where the citizens had raised money to further her singing training.

Port Pirie was another break for us, then Kalgoorlie. It was dusk and we took advantage of the optional bus trip around this thriving gold mining town. The following morning we arrived back in Perth after a really wonderful experience. We had visited New Zealand, renewed friendships with New Zealand and Sydney "Georges" and their families and spent special time with David. On our lavatory wall we had a large map of Australia, now we were able to really appreciate the size and contrast of this wonderful, vast country.

CHAPTER
THIRTY

The "Budgies" and Driving Lessons

Making preparations for the "Budgies" to arrive.
Welcome baby Stuart. I learned how to drive.

Don's Uncle Ernie, the cabinet maker who had made our treasured bedroom furniture, had a wife Elsie, three daughters and a son. The eldest daughter, Evelyn, I had known since she was ten. Now married with a small daughter, she and Mac were interested in emigrating. We gave them a lot of information and encouragement and in May 1971 welcomed them to Western Australia.

Immediately on arrival here, Evelyn dropped the "lyn" and has always been known as Eve. This is often confusing with two of us and everyone presumes she is *my* cousin. Australia is a land of abbreviations. We didn't realise when we named our son that we would have an "'ollyday"! Actually he strictly discouraged anyone shortening his name and it was only used temporarily by a few school friends.

Initially Eve, Mac and two-year-old Claire stayed with us. The adults slept on the couch that converted into a rather restricted, uncomfortable double bed. Eve was quite tall and Mac a big man, how they managed, I don't know. After a couple of weeks they found a small house to rent and the following year bought one in Armadale not far away. "Guess what?" Eve said with a big grin on her face soon after arrival, having visited the doctor, "I'm pregnant!"

Baby Stuart, conceived in England, was born in Australia the following January.

Oliver now nearly seven was Claire's great hero. She was a dear little girl and followed him everywhere plaintively calling "Oiver, Oiver". They became very good friends as we all did. It was wonderful to have some family here. (I did contact a remote, probably fourth, cousin of mine soon after arrival as they had immigrated some years previously. After our initial introduction to Peter, Muriel and family we rarely saw them.) Eve and I became very close friends and have remained so. Mac, a very amiable man got on with us all. He eventually found employment as an optical technician, continuing his chosen occupation. Many years later Claire followed in her father's footsteps and became similarly qualified. They missed their parents and siblings in England but being young and very sociable, assimilated easily.

Their presence coloured our lives in many ways. We enjoyed various outings together, Christmas became a family event and we had plenty of fun times. Once we organised a surprise fortieth birthday party for Bobby Bear, Cousin Eve's ancient and much loved teddy bear. We participated in each other's celebrations and it was

171

a joy to watch their children as well as ours grow and thrive.

When Claire was quite small and asked her full name, she couldn't pronounce Burgess and said "Budgie". From that day, they have been known affectionately as "the Budgies".

The first big event after our return from New Zealand was Stuart's arrival, the second was hearing that a friend of mine was taking driving lessons. I was flabbergasted. Like me, she had been a nervous passenger and I could never have visualised her or myself in the driver's seat.

"If she can do it, maybe I can?" I said to a surprised Don. I studied and passed the written test. No problems there, but being in control of a vehicle petrified me. The most terrifying moment of my life was that first time I sat with the instructor and turned on the ignition. My tutor, a Mrs Angel, did not live up to her angelic name. "Take your bloody foot off that sodding clutch."

I can still hear her roaring at me. She must have been a good teacher. After twelve lessons she told me she had arranged for me to have my test.

"It will be good practice for you, you will know what to expect," she told me. I told no one I was even attempting this intimidating challenge. The examiner had just failed a lady for the sixth time and spent the time grumbling about her. To my amazement and also consternation, I passed the test first time. I phoned Don, "I'm going to throw those L plates away."

"A good idea," he said.

Like me he thought I was far too daft to pass.

"Yes," I said "I've passed my driver's test."

"What?" he asked surprised "Well, I'll be buggered."

I now had my licence and was able to occasionally drive Don's car. This was not a good idea as I was scared of having an accident, however minor, in a car that was not mine. I was soon able to buy a car in reasonable condition and I could then feel more relaxed when driving, but far from confident.

Many years later at a seminar we were invited to share the most important event of our life. Many said their wedding day, some said the first time they held their baby, others when they graduated. My very materialistic reply was the day I gained my driver's licence. It spelt *independence*.

CHAPTER
THIRTY-ONE

Hobbies, Interests and Pets

Quiz nights, philosophy, massage and Tai Chi.
Many cherished cats and dogs, some with pedigree.

I have always been a bit of a "hobby butterfly" flitting from class to class in divers subjects. I enjoyed each one at the time.

Over the years I dabbled briefly and not very successfully in pottery, cake decorating, flower arranging and Chinese cookery. I was more successful at conversational French and later Italian. Possibly I have inherited my father's aptitude for languages. As an interpreter he spoke five.

I did a couple of courses at Technical College. One was Beauty Techniques. I was the only student aged over twenty, very much so, as I was in my fifties. The tutor asked my permission, willingly given, and used my face as an example of how skin deteriorates with age. I had all these lovely young girls peering at my skin under a powerful magnifier, rather disconcerting. My other tech. course was an introduction to philosophy;

stimulating classes with an excellent lecturer. I actually received good marks in the exam, I think it was the postscript I had written adapted from an old joke

Why is Eve's knowledge of philosophy like
   monogamy?
Because it leaves a lot to be desired.

Latterly I attended massage and reflexology classes, also aromatherapy and Reiki. These I have found enjoyable, stimulating and helpful, both for myself and others.

Once I won a prize at a Quiz night for a free class at our local Learning Centre. I had to choose something that was available when I was. I thought I would try a totally different subject and enrolled for greeting card making. I went for just one term but that inspired an absorbing hobby that has expanded. I find this interest so varied, satisfying and above all, useful.

I have always tended towards laziness when it comes to physical exercise. The gentle arts of yoga and Tai Chi attracted me and helped considerably to keep my hip flexible. After my operation when I was twenty-one, I feared I would always limp. I arrived in Australia complete with my reassuring walking stick. I have rarely used it. For various reasons I discontinued these disciplines.

Don and I enjoyed square dancing for a short time. In groups of eight, forming the square, one listened to the caller's command. This was not only fun but excellent exercise. It involved a good memory and co-ordination as we had to learn so many formal moves. I wore multiple stiff, frilly petticoats under my swirling skirt and Don wore a check shirt, unconventional attire for him. Sadly our group disbanded and Don did not want to travel far, so that was the end of a rare interlude in my life where we enjoyed the same pastime.

The only other one we have both enjoyed is attending Quiz nights. These are used as fund raisers and usually comprise tables of six or eight people who could pool their knowledge. The questions were usually on sport, music, literature or general knowledge. One I attended asked the question, "What does a dog do that a man steps into?" We had puppies at the time and I could only think of one thing. The answer was of course "pants". The quiz master followed this by asking, "What does a dog do that men drink?" That really had everyone puzzled. The answer — "whines"! Over the years we have been with various friends and have been lucky enough to win all sorts of prizes. I think one of the best was lunch at Parliament House Dining Room with Fred Tubby, Member of the Legislative Assembly for the electorate of Roleystone.

"I don't want to go there," grumbled Don. "Take someone else."

So I did. What a magnificent meal with impeccable service. The Premier ate at the adjacent table and I felt rather overawed by our surroundings. It did not spoil my usual hearty appetite. We actually won this prize again the following year.

Cats and dogs are not hobbies, but our pets have been a constant delight and interest. In England we had three cats at various times. Timmy our fluffy tabby, Shelley a tortoiseshell cat, followed by another tortoiseshell spotted white called Dominoes. Don had completely refused to consider a dog. I have always been an animal lover, particularly dogs. Soon after we arrived in Australia and the tabby kitten we found in the garden, Tiger Tim, had settled, we went to a church fête. The Tombola in Australia is called a Chocolate Wheel; maybe the prizes were originally chocolate? We won a puppy. A whole litter had been donated and other friends won one of these mixed breed pups. We named him Bonzo but from the beginning he was weird. We took him for his routine immunisation and soon after the vet advised having him "put to sleep". I never knew dogs could have psychosis. We were all bitterly disappointed. The others from the litter were all problem free.

To ease the pain, a friend gave us an adorable tortoiseshell kitten. Daisy lived with us until she was seventeen years old. I really loved that cat and she loved everyone, particularly babies. If a small child visited us, she appeared and allowed it to pull her tail, grab her and hopefully stroke her. Soon after her arrival she was pregnant. We allowed her to have one litter before having her spayed, as all our cats have been. She produced four pure white bundles of fluff whom we facetiously named Gladys, Ethel, Bert and Fred. They all went to good homes where they were very promptly renamed.

Sadie, an affectionate short haired tabby, arrived soon after, followed by Lulu. She had an aristocratic mien and just loved Oliver. He would wear her around his neck like a scarf — I had always wanted a grey cat. She was a real individual.

Fearless Fred completed our complement of four cats as Tiger Tim had long since died. We presumed he had as, like most of our cats when very old, he just disappeared. Fred was a large, rather aggressive ginger cat who shared his favours with a family up the hill. If we were roasting chicken, Fred appeared, bashed up any female cat that dared to be in his way and deigned to eat some of the chicken. The son of his "other" family informed us "he brought us a duck once". When we moved, I happily bequeathed Fred to them permanently.

"I know Bonzo was a disaster but I'd really love a dog, a pedigree one this time so that we can know its background," I begged Don. In the more relaxed lifestyle of Australia he succumbed. I was working and had saved enough to buy Mischa.

I was not very knowledgeable about various breeds and their characteristics, but I knew I liked and admired the beauty of Shetland Sheepdogs. Shelties, as they are affectionately called, are miniature Collies and to my besotted eyes enchanting. Mischa, a sable and white bitch, was fully grown when I bought her but only eight months old. Her pedigree was impeccable, and from the start she was *my* dog.

She had such a good pedigree I decided to breed from her. She was not a very sexy bitch but did produce one litter of beautiful puppies. Our obsolete shower recess in the laundry housed the whelping box with a notice on the door "Maternity Ward". I was the only one who attended her and the pups for the first twenty-one days. Then, as if by magic, little slits appeared in their closed eyes and soon they could see and also hear. Until I bred dogs I had no idea they were deaf as well as blind for the first three weeks.

Then they emerged and everyone could play with them, and we did. They were adorable but we knew we had to part with them. By the time they went at six weeks they were thoroughly socialised. The children helped with the work involved and we bought our first colour television with the profits.

I had such a lot to learn. I knew little of the actual mating process which is unique to dogs and wolves. Often I had seen a male dog mounting a female, but for actual insemination to occur, they end up tail to tail facing in opposite directions. The first time I saw this I was amazed.

Mischa accompanied me to the Pre-school each day. I could hear the children say "Mrs Day is in the toilet" as Mischa guarded the door. Later, when I transferred to Kelmscott and she could not accompany me, we got a companion for her. Tessa, a little tricolour Sheltie, was known as a "brood bitch", never so happy as when pregnant or with puppies. She produced many beautiful litters. I had to learn all the protocol of dog breeding, registration and choosing a unique prefix. All my dogs were "Honeythorne" named after our English home.

Each pup named after a herb or spice such as "Bold Basil", "Marigold" or "Poppyseed".

Poppyseed, or Poppy as we called her, we decided to keep, as by then Mischa had sadly died. Poppy was sable and white like Mischa, not one of Tessa's many pups were tricolour like their mother. We had no problem selling them. They went to a variety of homes, from being used as a working dog on a farm or as pets, to being exported to Singapore. They love exercise but are a breed that could live in a flat. As they are by nature working dogs, they are easy to train, obedient and very amenable as well as being ornamental.

Poppy was a good looking puppy so I decided to show her. What a palaver that was. I had to learn the techniques of the show ring, all the rituals, and cope with the fierce competition. I entered Poppy in the puppy section, won first prize and the coveted blue ribbon. Once only was enough for me. I found the whole system too "bitchy" and I don't have the strong competitive urge. No more showing, I decided.

"Please, Mum, are we going to have more puppies?"

The children delighted in them as much as I did so we bred from Poppy and Tessa. Although she was her daughter, Poppy was the "boss dog", Tessa had always been submissive. Both were much loved pets as were all our animals; they each were an indispensable part of our family life.

CHAPTER
THIRTY-TWO

Church Involvement

Decisions for the new church, at Mass I often read.
Majellan friendships and Retreats fill a vital need.

Both my parents were Jewish. Their arranged marriage had been a very happy one. Dad's father, who died long before I was born, had been the much loved Rabbi of Dover from 1860 until 1910. My maternal grandfather had the honour of being corsetière to King Edward VII.

As a small girl I had been brought up Jewish but was influenced by the many families with whom I had lived. My very insecure childhood was due to various factors, including the Blitz and my mother's death.

During my teenage years I knew I wanted to become a Roman Catholic but was not finally received into the church until I was twenty-two. Don was not a Catholic.

In England, apart from helping to clean the church, I was too busy rearing my young family to do more. It was very different in Australia where I soon became deeply involved in Parish commitments.

My faith has given me far more than I could ever repay.

The first day we attended church in Australia, the girls and I were all wearing our hats as we would have done in England. To my relief I saw only one elderly Italian lady with her head covered, everyone else was bare headed. Goodbye to fancy hats.

After a couple of months when I had got to know a few people I was surprised and flattered when the Parish Priest, Father Brian Harris, said, "Eve, I would like you to do the readings at Mass next Sunday?"

Initially I was intimidated by this responsibility but once I knew what to do, I enjoyed the privilege.

"Oh Mum," said my embarrassed children, "you sound as if you are telling a story to kindergarten children."

The congregation did not seem to mind. I had the honour of being the first woman reader in our Parish.

One Sunday a few years after our arrival, I had just finished reading when we all heard a fearful crash. A local butcher had suffered a heart attack whilst driving along the adjacent Highway. His car had veered off the road, slid down the embankment and crashed into the side of the church. No parishioners were hurt in this tragic incident, just very shocked. The poor butcher was dead at the wheel.

This solid church had been built in 1912 and was far too small for the rapidly growing community. Decisions were made to build a new one that was consecrated in 1976. Being the only woman on the building committee, my main contribution was the suggestion of a small room adjacent to the main structure where parents could attend the services with crying or disruptive children without disturbing the congregation. We held many discussions with the church authorities, financial committee and architects. We visited a number of churches in the metropolitan area and each selected factors that we approved of, or didn't. Some churches had a spiritual atmosphere as soon as one entered, in some I felt nothing.

We finally decided on a homestead design surrounded by verandas. Because of the sloping site, the building was raised to provide parking in the undercroft.

I spent a few years on the Parish Council in its early days and also was involved in Baptism preparation.

The dearth of priests, plus the expanding population, meant the necessity of the laity taking on increased responsibilities within the church.

A rare event occurred in the Roman Catholic Church in Western Australia in 1969. Three married Anglican ministers were ordained Catholic priests. Pope Paul VI approved this. Armadale made international history in 1973 by having the first married parish priest in the world.

Father John Lisle who had led a most interesting and dedicated life became our new priest. He and his devout wife Mary sadly only stayed one year. His health was not good and our geographically very large parish included two outlying country areas, very demanding.

The Presbytery had been modified to become a family home so his colleague, Father Geoff Beyer, succeeded him. He arrived with his charming wife Dorothy, a teenage daughter and three teenage sons.

183

Some of the older, more rigid parishioners found it very hard to accept a married priest when Father Lisle arrived, but now there was less antagonism. Father Beyer was a rather reserved, intellectual man; I also found him to be a very understanding, wise, compassionate counsellor. It is not many priests who would have had the privilege of marrying their daughter.

A popular Irishman, Father Jim Corcoran succeeded Father Beyer, who in turn was followed by Father Tony Pires. Tall, dark and handsome as well as being devout, he is blessed with a charisma appreciated by both adults and children.

For some years I had the reputation of being the church jester. It all started when we were enjoying a celebratory Majellan meal at the local Chinese restaurant. Recently returned from a holiday visiting friends in England I had been entertained there by a book of jokes with a religious bias. Seated next to Father Tony I told him about the little boy saying grace.

"The parents were expecting some important guests for dinner. When everyone was seated, Mother said to Johnny, 'Would you like to say grace for us, please?'

" 'Huh?' he replied.

" 'You know,' his mother said, trying to impress the guests. 'What did Daddy say before breakfast?'

" 'Oh, I remember,' answered Johnny. 'Oh God, are those awful people coming this evening?' "

Father was delighted.

"Eve," he said "have you any more jokes like that?"

"Lots," I replied.

184

"Please write this one out to be published in next week's newsletter, it is good to have a little humour."

From that day, "Eve's Corner" became a popular feature. I took the responsibility seriously and scoured libraries and bookshops both in Australia and overseas, being most particular that the jokes were suitable. I was careful to check that nothing would offend anyone. Occasionally people of other denominations visited and children often read these jokes.

"Why do we say A-men and not A-women?" she asked.

"Because we sing 'hymns' and not 'hers'," he replied.

"How old are you, Grandma?" asked little Jane.

"Oh, I don't know, dear," smiled Grandma. "I've had so many birthdays I've lost count."

"Well, why don't you look in your knickers?" said Jane, "mine say 4–5 years old."

After this one was published, I had a disconcerted man approach me.

"Oh dear," he said, "I must be older than I thought. My 'undies' say 105!"

By far the biggest influence on my settling happily in Australia was the local Majellan group. Named after the Patron Saint of Mothers, St Gerard Majella, these groups were founded in Perth in 1958. A childless lady, Eileen Honner saw the need for mothers, often of large families, to have an outlet. Majellans involve absolutely no demands, no fundraising, no expectations, no particular skills, and no commitments, just to *be*.

Our monthly meetings and membership over the years varied. We had speakers on religious topics,

185

homemaking themes, intellectual subjects, whatever the group felt in need of. Often we had no topic, just warm, intimate discussions. Many of us have been helped considerably by sharing our experiences, troubles and joys.

The bi-annual weekend Majellan Retreats became an important part of my life. Once Oliver reached the age of nine and no longer needed me for a bedtime story (although he had long been a fluent reader), I was able to attend these events that could be both stimulating and relaxing. Don and the children managed happily without me as they did when I went overseas. Chocolate biscuits were always on their celebratory menu.

Over the years I have found these Retreats had a huge influence on and benefit to me, apart from something to look forward to twice a year.

Firstly, the spiritual content. Each Retreat has a different spiritual director. Sometimes it is a Priest or a Brother or often a Nun, occasionally a lay person. Each one brings their own ideas, personality and skills to share with us. One Nun offered a foot massage during our free time on Saturday afternoon. The response was so overwhelming that I helped her. Naturally some of these directors have appealed to me more than others, but there is usually some reassuring advice or saying one remembers, such as St Julian of Norwich's "All will be well."

Secondly, I always enjoy just being away, a break from routine. The convent is just forty minutes drive in an attractive coastal suburb. We each have our own bedroom and are fed generously by the nuns. One can walk on the quiet beach and in the evenings the sun setting over the waters of the Indian Ocean is a magnificent and calming experience.

Thirdly and most importantly, the fellowship. There is something unique, intimate and special in these gatherings of about thirty like-minded women of various ages, some indefinable bond. Occasionally we have had a lady from another denomination join us. They gain as much as any of us and always remark on the congeniality of the group. Saturday evening has traditionally been the time for a bit of fun. Sometimes a guitar appears and we all sing. Jokes are told, silly games played. Sometimes the Central Majellan Committee have prepared a skit as they did one year on the film "Sister Act". So, as well as being a time for reflection and prayer, there is always a great deal of therapeutic laughter.

For some years I was a member of this committee and one year was State Vice-President. The feast day of St Gerard Majella is October 16. It is pure coincidence that I had my first child on this date. All the Metropolitan groups in Perth joined to celebrate Mass at the Redemptorist Monastery in North Perth. Afterwards we all congregated in the quadrangle prior to enjoying supper. The air reverberated with the chatter of many voices renewing old friendships. I noticed that groups were moving in to the hall to eat. Anxious to join them, I was waylaid by my dear friend Annette who struck up an animated conversation.

Impatiently I listened to her and eventually she suggested, "Let's go in to supper."

"Yes, let's," I eagerly agreed.

I nearly collapsed with shock as I walked in to the hall. Three hundred women burst into "Happy Birthday to you". It was actually my fiftieth birthday. On the podium hung a beautiful handmade banner "Eve, 50 years in His love". Below on a table stood a magnificent floral arrangement and the most gorgeous, huge cake with in gold lettering *Happy Birthday Eve Majellans*.

Someone shouted, "Speech, speech."

For once in my life I was speechless. I stammered "Thank you, th-th-thank you" in a state of delighted shock.

"Cut the cake," called another voice.

My heart sank. I was used to children bringing a sponge cake to the Pre-School to be divided into thirty-six, but three hundred!

"No, no, let her take it home," said another voice, to my great relief. I did and invited all the Central Committee to our next Majellan meeting where I cut and shared it ceremoniously. What wonderful friends to be blessed with.

CHAPTER
THIRTY-THREE

Voluntary Work

S.E.S. and patterning, Gumnut Guides are fun,
Birthright and S.V.P., help for everyone.

Over the years I have been fortunate to be able to help others in various voluntary capacities.

Some years ago a lady asked for volunteers to help to "pattern" her little Down's Syndrome baby. I phoned her.

"What is 'patterning'?" I asked.

"It is helping to perform passive exercises, but we need teams of three people, it is not hard work," she assured me.

I went. Each Wednesday her mother held the baby's head to one side then the other as two of us flexed the relative arm and leg. This is known as homolateral patterning.

The dedicated parents had visited Pennsylvania in the United States to attend the Institute for the Achievement of Human Potential. The director, Glen Doman, was the same man who had written the popular book "Teach Your Baby to Read'" that I used with Oliver. An individual programme was designed for each child using the cybernetic system of sensory-motor stimulation. This helped activate the brain and its neurons, developing increased intellectual ability, and is used for many brain-injured people.

This energetic, determined mother gave the toddler constant repetitive information. I remember watching this dear little girl, aged about two and half, being prompted to say "Butt-er-flies and moths are lepi-dopt-era" when shown a picture of them. Her parents put enormous effort into stimulating every aspect of her senses. I heard she attended a local primary school. I wonder how she is coping with life.

Later I joined Birthright, an organisation that helped lone parents, usually mothers. I befriended a particular family and took the mother and her two little girls on outings and remembered their birthdays with small gifts. Many of these women had fled from disastrous and often dangerous partnerships and frequently had no one to turn to. I did a lot of listening. Sadly, our local Birthright branch disintegrated.

The Local Voluntary Emergency Service — later known as the State Emergency Service — asked for volunteers for their Welfare section. We were issued with a smart uniform and attended meetings to organise the necessary support when a team of volunteers was called to an emergency. I remember making endless cups of tea in the bush as they searched for a small boy who had wandered off from a family picnic. Fortunately in that case there was a happy ending as the men were helped by the family dog. Not all the searches ended as

190

happily. We were a united, sociable group who remained good friends.

For a while I helped Carrie run the local "Gumnuts". These newly formed groups were for the youngest members of the Girl Guide movement, starting when they were aged six. I had been involved with five year olds for so many years this was no great step. Granddaughter Katie was in the group.

I will never forget the State's first birthday celebration in beautiful King's Park in Perth. One extremely hot February day saw all the Metropolitan Gumnut Guide groups gather for a day of fun. Carrie was unable to come so I went with the little girls and their parents. They had been told to bring their bathers and happily ran in and out of the spray from the sprinklers whilst we adults sweltered. We enjoyed our picnic under the large shady trees and an enormous celebratory teddy bear cake was cut. In the afternoon games had been organised, including a race for the leaders. I think I came last, I have never been so hot and exhausted in my life. It was most gratifying to hear that the temperature that day had been a record 44°C (114°F). What a day to run races.

I have offered my massage skills to various groups and given welcome foot massages to a group of carers of people with dementia. Most of these were spouses and all very dedicated to this demanding and often demoralising responsibility.

My longest lasting involvement has been with the local St Vincent de Paul Conference. We have a very dedicated, consolidated group of men and women.

Each day we visit local folk in their homes, of any or no denomination, who are in emergency need. We always go in pairs and try to help them with food, clothing, essential furniture and advice. Often a sympathetic ear is needed as much as a wardrobe. The people we visit vary. Sometimes they may have suddenly become unemployed and don't know where to turn until they receive financial assistance. Some just cannot manage their money and probably never will. Some are white, some aboriginal, some single, some married, and some in partnerships. Many are supporting mothers; some have husbands in jail. The homes we visit can vary between immaculate and squalid. The reaction we get from the people can fluctuate between aggressive presumption and genuine gratitude. The aid we give is emergency help, not a regular handout, and we constantly remind ourselves that we are there to help, not to judge.

Each fortnight the group meets for spiritual nourishment and discussions on various aspects of the society. We also address any particular problems we may have encountered with the people we visit.

A vital asset of our particular Conference is the fact that a few times a year we share a meal. We are not only volunteers in a very worthwhile cause, but friends.

CHAPTER
THIRTY-FOUR

617 Squadron

617 Squadron's Golden Jubilee.
Propitious celebrations, I'm sure you will agree.

Soon after our arrival in Australia, Phil said, "Come on, it's time you met the rest of the mob."

By this he meant the other members of the 617 Squadron often referred to as the Dambusters. At that time there were six living in Western Australia, including Phil and Don. The eldest was Lance, Jock was a Scotsman, Bob, and Tom who with his charming wife Susie had produced six children whose names all started with 'P'. Sadly only Don, Phil and Bob have survived.

We met fairly regularly those first few years at each other's scattered homes for an occasional barbecue. The men rarely talked about their traumatic wartime experiences except to laugh at the odd humorous incident. So many of their colleagues did not return from their sorties over Germany.

Some years later, Richard Todd, the star of "The Dambusters" film, visited Perth and invited the remaining crew members to lunch with him, a generous and thoughtful gesture.

A big event occurred on May 15th 1993, the fiftieth anniversary of the bombing of the Mohne and Eder dams. The Governor of Western Australia held a Ball in Government House in honour of the Dambusters.

"Oh dear," said Don, who by now had thoroughly acclimatised to Australian traditions and enjoyed wearing casual clothes, "I'll have to wear a dress suit — ugh."

He hired one and looked extremely smart and distinguished. The invitation had stated "full dress with medals", so he wore his miniatures. I wore a full length dress in teal, quite plain, with turquoise necklace and earrings.

After pre-prandial drinks served by extremely smart young trainee pilots in the large foyer of Government House, we were ushered into the magnificent ballroom. Circular tables, each seating ten, were placed down each side. The red carpet ran down the centre of the room.

"Oh, look at the soldiers!"

I gazed above the stage, and in the gallery were the trumpeters in their scarlet and gold uniforms. The music for the evening was provided by the Royal Australian Navy Band. Male and female Air Force cadets formed the guard of honour, so all three Defence Forces were represented.

The five men of 617 Squadron who were the guests of honour and their wives sat at separate tables with various dignitaries. We sat with the Air Commodore and his wife.

We had barely introduced ourselves when the men were hustled into the foyer. Everyone stood as the cadets sprang smartly to attention for the trumpeter's fanfare. The State Governor and his wife, the Lord and Lady Mayoress of Perth and the British Consul General took their places. First the band played "Advance Australia Fair" followed by the familiar strains of the Dambusters' March.

Each squadron member in turn was presented to the Governor. First Phil, the pilot, then the bomb aimer Don, follower by three air gunners, Bob, Dave and Frank. Each man walked alone on the red carpet the length of the ballroom. I felt very proud as Don walked through the guard of honour and bowed to the Governor.

"I know it is a long time ago, Don, but well done."

To their surprise each man was handed a parcel containing a set of beautiful Italian crystal wine glasses. Our friend Leo later engraved each one of ours and Phil's to commemorate this auspicious day.

The red carpet was rolled up in preparation for the dancing which was interspersed between the courses of the delicious meal.

"Don, do we *have* to dance?" I asked in panic a few weeks before the event.

"I don't know, you'll have to if someone asks you," he replied.

Don has never danced and it was many many years since I had. Anxiously I practised at home in front of the television. I had borrowed a video tape "Ballroom Dancing for Absolute Beginners". I knew Government House would hardly boast a *vcr* and television with two footprints on the floor to guide me. My fears were unfounded, to my great relief I was not asked to dance and I thoroughly enjoyed my spectator role.

We had an unforgettable evening, many people asked Don for his autograph and I managed to get our programme/menu signed by the Brigadier and Naval Commodore as well as the Air Commodore.

Phil and May did not want to stay too late and drove us home, arriving just before midnight, so all was well after the ball and the car did not turn into a pumpkin.

The following day was just as exciting but in a less formal way.

"All right, you folk," said Phil as he deposited us home late that Saturday, "I'll collect you after lunch tomorrow to take you to Jandakot airport. You know we are to be the guests of honour at the Royal Aero Club."

"Thank goodness I don't have to wear the dress suit," said Don as I folded it carefully prior to returning it to the hire shop. He looked very smart in his blazer with the squadron crest; he wore his squadron tie too.

At Jandakot we assembled in a large hangar. Phil gave a briefing as he would have done fifty years previously.

Twenty-three light planes were flying the course preceded by three Macchi jets from the R.A.A.F. to pay tribute to the occasion. Don and the other 617 members climbed aboard the leading plane. Soon after, three of us wives boarded a little four-seater Cessna

196

182. I was so pleased I had the forethought to take my camera and took many aerial photos, good, bad and indifferent. We flew symbolically over Canning Dam and then, on our way to the City, we actually flew over our home. I could pinpoint it as it was so close to the hospital. The train resembled a tiny silver worm. How breathtaking flying over the City! The sun shone brilliantly on the river and the glass from the multi-storied buildings gleamed in the reflection. After an exhilarating fifty minute flight, we literally returned to earth. My fears of travel sickness were unfounded although I would not care to fly in a light plane during bad weather.

Back on "terra firma" we talked and had a few drinks, then to my delight viewed an aerobatic display by a formation of small planes, Chipmunks I think. Later we watched a solo pilot plane loop the loop and perform spectacular rolls for his admiring audience.

As dusk fell, we all moved into the Royal Aero Club. Here we had a delicious buffet meal. Speeches of thanks and acknowledgments were made and one gentleman gave an informative and interesting talk on Barnes-Wallis, the inventor of the bouncing bomb.

As soon as we returned home the phone rang. An excited Carrie had seen a brief segment of Don and the other 617 men talking in the ballroom on the television news.

What an exciting and unforgettable weekend.

CHAPTER
THIRTY-FIVE

Name Dropping

Faith Addis, Sylvia Syms. The names I drop are many. The U.S. Ambassador, Lord Wedgwood, "Little Penny".

At my penultimate boarding school, Annecy Convent in Seaford Sussex, I often helped Sister Barbara tuck the "babies" into bed and read to them. They were aged about six and I was sixteen. Each little bed had a different coloured doll-nightdress case residing on it and each little girl, treated as a cherished individual. One of these, "little Penny", became better known as the actress Penelope Keith. She retained her maiden name.

Some years ago whilst staying with my dear friend Maureen in England, she said, "Anywhere special you would like to visit?"

"Oh, let's go to Guildford, I'd like a sentimental trip to see the church where we were married and the Prince of Wales Hotel where the reception was held."

Alas, the church had been rebuilt elsewhere and the site now contained a high rise office block. No one knew the whereabouts of the hotel and I realised a large shopping centre now occupied that site. Progress is inevitable.

"Never mind," I said, "We'll have a look at the shops there."

On the ground floor there was a big commotion. A new food hall was to be opened. The Mayor and other dignitaries stood back to allow Penelope Keith, the guest of honour, cut the ribbon. We mingled with the appreciative crowd and to Maureen's great consternation, I left her watching and boldly walked up to Penelope. People clustered around her with autograph books. She smiled graciously at each fan as she signed.

"Hallo, Penny," I said. She spun round surprised. No one called her Penny now.

"You won't remember me, but I used to tuck you up in bed when you were a little girl at Annecy."

"Did you, my deah?" her smile now genuine delight. We chatted for a while — like me, she still kept in touch with the dear nuns at the convent. She gave me some of the latest gossip. I felt so disappointed that I had no autograph book. I always carry a little notebook with me and asked her to sign that, telling her how popular she was in Australia. I treasure that piece of paper — "To Eve. How nice to see you again. Good luck. Penelope Keith."

I had met Maureen at my final school and had a lot of explanations to make.

What a lucky coincidence I should be at that shopping centre that particular day.

Some years ago Sylvia Syms and Alfred Marks performed in the play "In Praise of Love" in Perth. She and I had shared a dormitory at my last school, Merrow Grange in Guildford Surrey. I invited her here but she said, "I'm sorry, my time is limited but come back stage after the show and we'll meet there."

Her beautiful features had not changed. Alfred Marks strode in scratching his crotch. "You'll have to forgive me, I'm a chronic balls scratcher."

Cousin Eve had accompanied me back stage and our laughter set the scene for a happy half-hour's reminiscing.

Whilst in London, I accompanied Vicki, Bernhard's wife, to Lillywhite's, the prestigious sports shop in the West End. She needed some good walking shoes. I gaped, there opposite us was a handsome man with a young girl who was trying on tennis shoes.

"Look," I said amazed, "isn't that the actor Tom Conti?"

"Oh yes," replied Vicki casually, "hallo Tom" and she introduced me.

"However do you know him?" I asked.

"His wife Kara, a talented artist, gives a group of us lessons in their home. Tom always makes the coffee." Vicki too was very skilled.

Just a few years ago there was a big Wedgwood promotion at the Parmelia Hotel in Perth. I had received an invitation to see the latest products and hear Lord Wedgwood speak. I went straight after my French class, and took my camera.

"Could I please take a photo of you?" I asked him.

"Certainly you can," he shook my hand. I sympathised with him briefly over how weary he must feel after the long flight.

The following day I wrote this little rhyme in honour of the event. I could hardly believe that some people thought me sacrilegious when they heard the title.

THE LORD'S DAY

Here's a little incident of which I'd like to brag
It happened to me after class last week.
I have a little camera, I keep it in my bag,
It was in there when I heard Lord Wedgwood speak.
I'd gone to the Parmelia, it wasn't far to walk,
I knew there would be sandwiches and wine.
The history of Wedgwood was a most inspiring talk
And afterwards we glimpsed each new design.
Later as Lord Wedgwood walked towards the door,
I photographed him, then was over-awed
When he shook my hand and chatted,
I'll not wash it any more.
So I'm bragging of the day I met the Lord.

Western Australia was rightly proud of having built the replica of Captain Cook's barque the *Endeavour* in 1993. Its first ocean voyage was to be from Fremantle to Albany, a charming town and port in the extreme south west.

Great festivities were planned for her arrival and a special train travelled from Perth for the celebrations.

201

This caused extra excitement as the passenger service had been discontinued many years previously.

Preparing for an adventurous retirement, this was my first lone enterprise, just a weekend away.

The Heritage train was lovingly maintained and staffed by dedicated volunteers. As we boarded we were given tickets and table numbers for first or second lunch. I love October, the autumn colours in England and the spring in Australia. Here everything blossoms profusely. We passed trees of yellow wattle, red eucalypt blossom and the paddocks were still green from the winter rains. The journey was long but enjoyable. I have always loved train travel.

"First sitting for lunch, first sitting for lunch."

The announcement had everyone, about fifty people, in my long carriage disappear toward the dining car. Alone I sat, appreciating the silence except for the rumbling of the carriages. The lady sitting next to me returned after a while and told me about the beautiful dining car and meal. Soon I heard, "Second sitting for lunch, second sitting for lunch."

The dining car *was* beautifully laid out with a number of small tables attractively decorated with tablecloths and flowers. My table number just wasn't there. Oh dear, what now? The supervisor arrived and directed me to another carriage immediately behind the engine. Here I found to my surprise a large table elegantly set for ten people. An attentive waiter showed me to my place. Alone only briefly, an elderly man and young woman soon joined me. Then a handsome American negro sat opposite me and introduced

202

himself as Edward, his attractive wife was Lucy and their teenage daughter Sarah sat between them. Next to me sat another American couple Dan and Ros. The two men the far end of the table were not introduced.

We enjoyed the delightful meal and had cursory conversation hampered by the jolting of the train and the very noisy diesel engine. It was a pleasant interlude.

On arrival at Albany, a band to welcome us greeted the train and the station was decorated with bunting for the occasion. We huddled together awaiting the buses that would take us to our respective motels.

"Did you know the United States Ambassador to Australia, Edward Perkins, and his family were on the train?" the news spread fast.

"And the West Australian United States Consul Dan Duffy and his wife Ros."

Amazed I realised I had been chosen to dine with them, I have no idea why. I then gathered that the two unidentified men had been bodyguards.

A dear friend and fellow Majellan from Armadale, Josie, and husband Lindsay were staying in Albany in their caravan that week. She knew of my trip and concerned for my spiritual welfare, had said "If you like, we'll collect you from your motel on Saturday evening and take you to Mass with us."

I agreed, happy to see familiar faces. We went to the attractive new church and I was admiring the architecture when the priest went to the lectern and announced, "Fellow parishioners, we are very honoured this evening to have Edward Perkins, the United States Ambassador, attend Mass here with his family." All heads turned. In procession walked Edward, Lucy and Sarah. He caught my eye. There was a small wave of acknowledgement and his face lit up with a broad smile of recognition. Josie turned to me in amazement.

"Do you know him?"

"Oh yes," I replied casually, savouring the moment "I had lunch with him yesterday!"

I read a wonderful series of autobiographical books starting with "The Year of the Cornflake" by Faith Addis. Her book "Down to Earth" was the basis of the television serialisation. After reading her third book I was motivated to write and tell her how much I enjoyed her memories and to sympathise with her fear of spiders. I mentioned I would shortly be visiting the West Country and would love to try the Devonshire Teas she mentioned in the book. Her reply informed me that her Devonshire Tea business had come and gone. They were then living in Newton Abbott, Devon. She sent me her phone number and the tempting invitation "the kettle is always on".

A few months later, whilst staying with Doug and Ronnie in Somerset, I phoned her and received complicated instructions to find her home. Ronnie and I eventually drove down the narrow lane to a warm welcome. The two ladies looked at each other.

"I know you," said Ronnie.

"I know *you*," Faith was laughing.

A few years previously they had both belonged to the same Smallholders Association. Faith's two delightful dogs Honey and Parsley, who featured strongly in her books, were very much part of the family. We chatted as if we were old friends, casual and very relaxed.

This event was fifteen years ago. The seed of my intention to write had not then been sown. I knew I could never attempt writing my memories, as I was unable to type. Faith was my inspiration when she told me, "I write all my books in ball point pen and pay to have them typed."

Amazed, I valued this information, so potent that eventually that seed germinated. Thank you, Faith.

CHAPTER
THIRTY-SIX

Pre-School

Reading stories, dressing up, meeting each new pet.
Little individuals I never shall forget.

(To save embarrassment I have identified the children by a random initial.)

I often think how fortunate I was to be employed for over twenty-five years in a job I really loved. Initially an aide at Armadale Pre-school for seven and a half years, I then worked at Kelmscott. The title was changed to assistant when the word aide became unacceptable. Later, when the Education Department took over from the Pre-school Board, we became known as a Pre-primary and were part of Kelmscott Primary school.

Each group of thirty-six children attended for four half days. The parents paid a small weekly fee for the privilege of giving the children this year of valuable preparation for school. At the start of each school year we had to learn seventy-two names — quickly. Later, when we became a Pre-primary, we had one less staff member and only twenty-five children in each group.

The children all had their fifth birthday during the year. It is a delightful age. They have not yet developed the complexities of school children, but are old enough to be independent and have definite characters. It is also an age when they are eager to please — well, usually.

I remained "pig in the middle" with Krysia the teacher in Armadale and Dorothy at Kelmscott. The assistants I worked with were Nancy and Margaret, each part time, and at Kelmscott, Shirley and Lilian.

In Australia we are fortunate that the children are able to play outside nearly every day. One year I counted the days when it was just too wet for them to play out at all and it was only nine. We had excellent adventurous outdoor equipment, the children always went barefoot outside. The only couple of broken bones I encountered during all those years were from children falling off a chair or a low log.

As well as their gross motor control, wc had a comprehensive programme to develop the whole child. No formal lessons, each Pre-school was autonomous. We hoped that by the time they started school they could write their name, count with understanding and know their colours, so many of the activities were focussed to develop these skills. Of course most of the children were far more competent than this minimum requirement.

As part of the programme, each year we visited the farm run by the local High school. A school bus collected us. We were shown the pigs, goats, sheep, turkeys and held the baby chicks. We watched the cow being machine milked, then could try ourselves. It was a really exciting, interesting morning. When we asked a child what he enjoyed most, "Ooo the ride on the bus," was the usual reply. These children were driven everywhere and rarely went on buses or trains.

During the seventies, playgroups were uncommon so often coming to Pre-school was the first time away from mother; most were ready and eager but a few were reluctant and showed it. I will never forget very irate twins trying to climb over the gate after their mother had said goodbye and wisely gone. They stood screaming so I took them each by the hand. G kicked me in the shins whilst S bit my bottom in his rage — no danger money in this job. After a day or two they settled happily. I would whisper a secret into a distressed child's ear.

"You're only here to play and have a good time. The teachers are all kind and Mummy will soon be coming for you — that is our secret."

"Can you whisper me our secret again?" they often begged.

I have always loved animals as well as children. Well, most animals. I had only been there a term when little N returned after a few weeks absence. She had accompanied her parents to the outback. They produced wonderfully photographed natural history books. This very shy child, as a mark of affection, tenderly placed on my chest a thorny devil. This horrific looking spiky creature is quite harmless but I nearly collapsed with shock at the time. Frogs were another creature I was unable to touch. I cleaned out

208

the mouse cage and handled the tame female but oh! that vicious male. I wore rubber gloves as I lifted him correctly holding the base of his tail. He swung round and sank his teeth into the glove; it was not easy to pry him free. He only stayed with us briefly as we were soon inundated with babies. The tiny, blind, naked, squirming bodies fascinated the children.

Guinea pigs made excellent pets and could become quite tame. The children sat outside in a circle as we passed one round to be gently stroked. One little girl, T, had many problems, including *no* speech. She loved animals. We told the children they had to say, "My turn please," before taking it from her neighbour. We passed T by, then the next time, to our amazement, we heard a rather hesitant, "My — turn — please," her first ever words. The power of animals.

Once the female guinea pig actually produced a litter of two whilst the children watched. Very different from baby mice as, after a few licks from mother, their fur soon dries and these miniature guinea pigs are running around, a real delight. A talent I possess is being able to sex the babies and occasionally I was called to use my ability at a neighbouring Pre-school.

Various animals have been brought in to visit us. Orphaned joeys (baby kangaroos), lambs, goats, kittens, even a pet rat. Sometimes a mother brought a real baby in to bath. The children loved this and it was particularly touching to watch little boys as well as the girls handle the baby so tenderly.

One area I didn't venture into was the aviary. We had a variety of colourful budgerigars, native to Northern

Australia. On my final day at the Pre-primary I lived up to my name of "Adamant Eve". Plucking up my courage I was determined to enter this innocuous cage. Since I was a child and had an unpleasant experience with bats, I hate anything fluttering around me.

At Armadale my dog Mischa had accompanied me each day. We had a birthday party for her. I distinctly remember the Vet's daughter bringing her a beribboned bone. Tessa only came with me to Kelmscott for her first birthday.

"Why isn't she blowing out the candle?" asked M.

"Because she needs you all to help her," was my swift retort.

Each September out came the silkworm eggs we had kept from the previous year. We scrounged the necessary mulberry leaves either from "Mrs Next-door" or a tree down the road. For five weeks they grow rapidly from a minute thread size until they are as big and fat as my little finger. They shed their skin four times during this process. Silkworms are very labour-intensive. Each day my job, helped by *sensible* children, was to pick the caterpillars very gently off the remnants of the old leaves and place them on to new ones. They spin their cocoon over a few days, moving their head in a figure of eight. An amazing two kilometres of silk is on each cocoon. The chrysalis then hatches in two weeks to produce a flightless moth. The larger female mates with the male who then promptly dies, as she does after laying between three and four hundred eggs and the whole cycle starts again the following September.

There are so many little characters to remember but a few stand out. We invited the fathers to come in the evening for an hour or two to play with their children, a very popular event. Each child painted a picture of him to decorate the walls. This was in the days when most children came from two parent homes.

"Come on J, paint a picture of Daddy," said Krysia.

"*No*, I don't *want* to."

He was a very strong willed but delightful, intelligent boy.

"Yes, you will," Krysia put a brush in his hand, "now paint."

He gritted his teeth, dipped the brush into the black paint and covered the paper.

"Thank you, J," Krysia said, "now tell me about it."

Never at a loss for an answer J said, "It's Daddy in the dark."

Another time we asked the children individually what these five-year-olds would do if they had lots of money. Most said they would buy lollies. One little fair-haired boy, the eldest of three, gave a surprising answer.

"I'd buy Mummy a new washing machine, ours is broken. I'd buy Daddy a new lawnmower and I'd buy D and P toys."

He never mentioned any desires of his own. Not surprisingly he has grown into a charming, happily married man.

One mother came in complaining, "B is using bad words. I don't know where the little sod is getting them from!"

One little boy S on his very first day would not answer his mother when she said, "Have you had a lovely day? What did you do?" He remained silent.

She was quite perturbed until he rushed to the sink on arriving home and spat out a mouthful of carrot. It had been there since "fruit time". It reminded me of the mouthful of plasticine I unwisely tasted as a child.

One delightful little girl never called us by name, it was always, "Heyyouknowwhat!"

Another boy, M, greeted me each day in his high-pitched voice. "You look very pretty, Mrs Day. I'm a *good* boy, aren't I, Mrs Day?"

I became very friendly later with his mother who helped me with my struggling Italian conversation.

Once someone donated a container of daffodil bulbs. We asked each child to bring in a pot.

"Does anyone know what a daffodil is?" asked Dorothy.

"Yes, I do," said P, "we spread it on our bread." (Daffodil is the name of a brand of margarine.)

We had a discussion on how useful our hands and fingers were. Many suggestions were made and after exhausting the obvious, little D raised his hand and said in his gruff voice, "I know, you can use your fingers for getting bogeys out of your nose."

Little R once had a ladybird land on her clothes.

"Isn't it pretty," she said, "I can see it is a ladybird and not a manbird."

One of my favourite series was the "My Naughty Little Sister" stories by Dorothy Edwards. No coloured pictures as most of the books had. I just read to them and told them, "You can shut your eyes if you like and see the pictures in your head." My mother's words to me, *many* years ago.

The children just loved these rather old fashioned stories and begged for them again and again. Many an adult I have spoken to reminds me saying, "How *is* your naughty sister? I remember the stories about her."

I often thought as I happily read or told the children stories, "My goodness, I am actually being *paid* to do this."

We often made crowns or party hats, children love dressing up. Once we were given a box of large feathers and made some quite dramatic Red Indian headresses using corrugated cardboard. As always, I wore one and, completely forgetting it was on my head, walked to the bank in my lunch hour wearing it. I should have greeted them "How!" Another Easter time we all made "bunny ears". I wore mine and hopped to the gate to greet the children in a pink track suit with cotton wool tail. I'm sure I embarrassed poor Dorothy, but the children loved it. I have never grown up!

Kelmscott Pre-school was an unusual design, a geodesic dome. It had its problems but was an interesting shape to work in. Occasionally a foul smell greeted us.

"Oh no," said Shirley, "I think there's a dead mouse somewhere."

We emptied the shelves in the large store cupboard. Chewed paper and mouse droppings verified our suspicions. Eventually we would find the putrid culprit — ugh! The attraction must have been the pasta we used for collage, always kept in a glass jar. A few years before retirement in 1993 the building was demolished. The Education Department replaced it with an ordinary rectangular demountable building. I felt really sad at the end of an era.

One year the fire engine arrived on its annual visit to be greeted by excited children. The tall handsome fireman who talked to the children said delightedly, "Do you know when I was five I used to sit on Mrs Day's lap!"

It gives me great pleasure to see the children grow up to be successful. One very bright girl predictably became a doctor, another very quiet, rather shy child is now one of our local librarians. She has blossomed.

Alas, very occasionally one can predict a child who will *not* be a success in life. One such boy, R, was very attached to me. I always like the challenging children. He loved to have his photo taken. Instead of running away at "mat time" he came in willingly if I had the camera, no matter it contained no film. A few years ago we heard he had made a dramatic escape from Fremantle jail and the car he stole was seen heading towards Armadale — for a photo?!

So many personalities over the years — I don't forget them and am delighted when a waitress may come up and shyly say, "Aren't you Mrs Day? Do you recognise me?"

The nurse at the hospital, the hairdresser, shop girl, physiotherapist — so many remember me. I have also been involved in many other local groups so it is not surprising I am recognised wherever I go.

One year we had a group of boys who were all potential leaders, causing a bit of friction, but on the whole the children all got on well. The staff were a happy team, never any bickering. For some years before retiring, I had the pleasure of the next generation. I had worked at Kelmscott congenially with Dorothy for twenty years and loved every minute of it.

CHAPTER
THIRTY-SEVEN

Holidays Overseas

Incurably nostalgic, I indulged my inclinations. Having many happy holidays with friends and our relations.

Some of the extra money I earned with my other jobs enabled me to have a number of holidays.

When I was very young we stayed at Westgate in Kent each year. Once I started boarding school at the age of seven I had no more holidays until I was grown up. I had never left England until we emigrated and in those days all I really yearned for was security. Now I was the other side of the world and being incurably nostalgic, I longed to see England's "green and pleasant land" and the many friends and relatives I had left. I needed to pluck up the courage to go alone as after our New Zealand holiday, Don was not keen on travelling.

I planned a trip to England in 1973 mainly to see dear Uncle Harry, my mother's brother. She was born on his third birthday and they had always been very close. When she died, I was eleven, and he promised her he would always care for me. He was an unforgettable, loveable character. Yes, I had a dear father but he was undemonstrative and rather introverted, the opposite of Uncle Harry. Sadly Uncle Harry died a couple of months before my intended departure.

"Are you still going?" Don asked.

I thought about it.

"Yes," I replied. "I've saved enough, the children are old enough to manage without me, I *will* go."

That first visit in the English spring revived my delight in all the familiar flowers. Primroses galore bloomed on the railway banks, the woods carpeted with bluebells, even a few cowslips were to be found in Somerset. I received a very warm welcome from the many people I visited. It was quite exhausting trying to spend a day or two with all those whom I missed but very rewarding, renewing the friendships.

I visited Aunt Bess. A very powerful figure, she loomed large in my childhood and I had always been in awe of her. After her first husband was killed in a tram accident she married Uncle Bob, a handsome Canadian doctor over twenty years her junior. She had been married over twenty-five years to her first husband, and to Uncle Bob over forty. She was childless. I visited this formidable lady and asked her

"How old are you now, Auntie?" to which she replied, "You never ask a lady her age!" End of subject.

Only three years later she delightedly sent the newspaper cuttings of the party and the telegram for her hundredth birthday. From that day, whenever she felt a bit "frail", she had a nip of whisky and, according to cousin Marcelle, consumed quite a quantity before she died aged over one hundred and one.

One thing I really missed was English Marmite, a different taste from the Australian product. It is produced in a distinctive heavy glass jar, rather weighty in my luggage. On my first return visit I bought a small jar and dutifully declared it at Customs. Australia is rightly very strict about food imports. Marmite is made from yeast, no meat extracts, so was cleared without any problems. Subsequently on later visits, I scraped the Marmite from the breakable jar into a lightweight Tupperware container and never even bothered to declare it.

"It's all right, Mum," Oliver reassured me when I told him. "You could always have said it was Aboriginal face cream!"

Australia, I believe, is the only country in the world that gives three months fully paid long service leave to its Federal and State government employees. Even a humble Pre-school assistant qualified. Some departments offer it every seven years, some every ten. I qualified twice during my many years of employment. Don never took his — in those days it could be accumulated and taken as cash at retirement. He updated his car.

I became more adventurous with my travelling but still liked the security of being met on my arrival by a familiar face. I am not really happy going alone. One year a Majellan friend Kath, who had never visited England, joined me for a holiday to see faces and places.

218

My friends and relatives extended to her their warm welcome. This was a great opportunity to sightsee as well as renew friendships. During those five weeks we only needed five days "Bed and Breakfast". At last I was able to visit Scotland and Wales, if only briefly. The décor of the Welsh bed and breakfast was unbelievable and unforgettable. A blue and gold carpet with a large swirly pattern, red and cream regency striped wallpaper, the curtains had a large floral pattern predominantly mauve and yellow, and the tables were covered with green check tablecloths. Each item alone was pleasant enough but oh, the conglomerated chaos.

We wisely bought a Britrail pass that gave us three weeks unlimited travel on the railways and we certainly made good use of it.

Bernhard and Vicki's large home in North London included a small flat where we stayed, very convenient. They took us to see the Tower of London, Buckingham Palace and many of the sights. It was fun visiting most of the places on the Monopoly board which previously had been only names to Kath.

We went to Seaford to see the dear nuns who had taught me, also my teacher Isabel Dutton. She had not changed over the years, eccentric as ever. Her woolly, wiry hair now quite grey, she still dressed in tweed skirts and wore brogues. She said, "I'm afraid we haven't room for you to stay here but we have booked you both into the Seaford Head Hotel at our expense," so very kind of her.

"I have just come from teaching art to a group of elderly folk," she informed us. At the time she must have been about eighty.

She lived in a large detached house not far from the convent. Nothing had changed since I was there thirty years previously. The murky kitchen still had a deep earthenware butler sink and wooden draining board, no "fridge". The dark oak panelled dining room and chintz covered chairs in the sitting room were as I remembered them, no television. Isabel shared the house with her sister Mary and friend Rose. She suffered from the painful condition trigeminal neuralgia, causing acute pain to the side of her face. Mary, the housekeeper, cooked and cleaned. Recently, although in her eighties, she had been climbing a tree to pick some apples when the poor dear had fallen and broken her back. She was in constant pain. Rose, a lifelong friend, had lived with them for about fifty years. The chauffeur of the trio, she drove the elderly car with difficulty, also considerably dangerously! She had severe torticullis, which left her head dramatically turned to the right. Isabel sat in the passenger seat and gave her directions and instructions. These three devout elderly ladies led a very cloistered life.

That evening we shared a memorable meal with them in their over-ornate dining room. Mary, unable to sit with a fractured spine, reclined on a chaise longue, Isabel could not bite or chew her food so mashed it to a pulp and sucked it. Rose was quite expert at aiming her food around the corner to her mouth, but sometimes missed. The whole scene could have been from a cartoon. I felt guilty seeing the humour of the situation, they were such gracious, genuine, loveable people.

A few years later I visited them again, alone this time. Isabel had an amazing memory considering the number of pupils she had taught. She recollected that the subject of my essay for School Certificate had been "My Books". A very talented teacher, she had us perfect three essays which could have been easily adapted to a wide variety of subjects. She knew of my weakness and insisted on giving me some of her very old treasured books. I do mean *old*, one is dated 1614. I felt guilty accepting them, but in retrospect realise she knew I would cherish them and she had no relatives to leave them to. That particular visit coincided with the tragic assassination of Lord Mountbatten. They had borrowed a small television to watch the funeral and sat around it entranced and twittering like a group of excited schoolgirls.

On my first long service leave I bought a "Round the World" ticket. My first stop was a week in New Zealand briefly seeing David and family, and Joy and George. I then travelled via Hawaii to San Francisco. It sounds very adventurous but I had pre-booked my hotel and taxi. The next day I flew via Chicago to Toronto where my cousin Jill met me. It was over forty years since we had seen each other but she was definitely recognisable. I guess I looked quite a bit different from the ten year old she remembered. She and Saul gave me a wonderful welcome to their charming farm in nearby Orangeville.

221

Many years ago I received a letter from a Dutch lady called Marina Barnstijn. Now living in Canada, she had married a distant cousin on my father's side. She was researching his family to produce a book on its history. I willingly gave her what information I knew and we kept in touch regularly. Like Australia, Canada is a vast country but I discovered they only lived an hour's drive from Jill. She invited them over for lunch, and meeting Hans I could definitely see some family resemblance.

One of our outings was a visit to Niagara Falls. It poured with rain and I felt distinctly queasy on the long drive. We stopped at a public lavatory at my request and I shall never forget the shock. There were the Falls. I hadn't realised we were so near nor their immensity, an unforgettable experience.

Jill had played an important part in my childhood as someone I admired and who gave me encouragement.

I flew from Toronto to Heathrow and spent more happy weeks seeing my many friends and particularly Don's relations and wallowed in the culture and history of my native land.

On my way home I had booked a week in Hong Kong where Don joined me reluctantly. Once there, he thoroughly enjoyed the new experience of a different environment as he did the time he met me for a week in Singapore. Once, on my own during a Hong Kong stopover, I had an unforgettable day trip into China. Most of the sightseeing was strictly organised but we were "set free" in some markets for an hour. I wandered away from the group, past the drab clothing stalls to the food area. To my horror I saw dog being

222

sold for meat. Ugh! I couldn't cope. I fled back to our designated meeting place and found the primitive lavatory where I promptly vomited.

I also had stopovers on my own in Singapore on other trips. It is possibly one of the few places in the world where a woman could travel alone safely. How different from the rather smelly claustrophobic city I remembered. The improved drainage system had almost removed the objectionable odour. Large international stores abounded. My delight were the small stalls with various goods one could bargain for — and I did.

My distant cousin Sophie, a retired barrister, and I had a week in Amsterdam during their Floriade. This is only held every ten years and was a spectacular experience. We went on the canals and a highlight of the trip was a visit to Hoorn where my paternal grandfather was born.

School friend Maureen, also my godmother when I was received into the Roman Catholic Church, accompanied me to Rome one year for a short holiday. We stayed near the station and within walking distance of many of the wonderful historical churches and monuments. To visit the Vatican we needed to travel on the incredibly crowded bus.

For someone who had never ventured away from the small area of England I knew, my horizons had widened. After leading a very insular and restricted life, even though my childhood had such diversity, I now loved the adventures of travelling. I enjoyed seeing how other people lived, their culture and of course their *food*.

On one memorable English holiday I had the great privilege of a visit to Glyndebourne. This prestigious Opera House in Sussex is privately owned and only the best singers perform there. Basil, a long time family friend whose friendship I had recently renewed, was a member. Even then, tickets were only available via a lottery.

Traditionally, sophisticated picnic suppers are enjoyed on the meticulous spacious lawns. A fascinating experience, seeing tables set with starched cloths, sparkling cutlery, candelabra and exotic food. We had a superb meal in the restaurant. Evening dress was compulsory and Basil had been most anxious.

"Remember, Eve, you *must* pack a long dress."

The environment, the other guests and the sense of occasion were more memorable than the performance of Handel's opera "Theodora", *not* a favourite of mine. Basil was delighted with my enthusiasm and appreciation of this unique treat.

"I've been to Glyndebourne!"

CHAPTER
THIRTY-EIGHT

Other Jobs

Tupperware and massage, different avenues. Work for Market Research, lots of interviews.

When I transferred to Kelmscott Pre-school after I left full time employment at Armadale, it was a part-time job. Initially I worked half a day, every day, but later this was changed to two full days and half a day, giving me two free days. This I found to be a happy compromise as I was able to *live* as well as work. An assistant only earned a small wage and now it was halved. I have always been aware that if one wants something in life, one must work for it, so I looked for other casual employment.

I decided to try Market Research. The company interviewed me in Perth and, after a short period of training, found me suitable. I interviewed people in shopping malls or centres but mainly door to door.

I spent a few years interviewing people in their homes on various specific topics such as new housing, insurance, medical products or confectionery. I drove to many unfamiliar suburbs and became an adept map-reader. I often needed to knock on many doors in my designated area before I found a suitable client.

"Good morning. I am Eve from . . . Market Research. Can you spare a few minutes to answer some questions on . . .?"

Often people were out or slammed the door in my face. I met many people who were lonely and greeted me eagerly to relieve their boredom, but often did not fall into the necessary category — such as "female aged under fifty". It could be tedious and frustrating but I was well paid and met some interesting and fascinating people. Once, when I arrived during a bad storm, a dear old gentleman insisted that I sat at the table with him and gave me a bowl of soup while I questioned him. It is only in retrospect that I realise with horror how very vulnerable I was. Often I entered a house with only one or two men present. Once when I had to find a male smoker, I had knocked on endless doors and was delighted to be greeted by a young man, cigarette in mouth. I interviewed him on his doorstep as I could see half a dozen men inside smoking and drinking beer.

Sometimes, in a shopping precinct, I invited passers-by to answer the questions. On one memorable occasion a local ice-cream firm had produced a new "ice confection". I was given three cartons of ice-cream (in a cooler box) labelled A, B and C. I soon had a crowd around me eager to taste and rate their preference. After one hour I was able to pack up and take the remnants home for willing consumption there. I never knew what A, B and C were, but knew C was the most popular and delicious.

Market Research was a new experience for me. It broadened my horizons, my abilities and most of all my self-confidence. I have never lacked initiative but have always been rather reticent with strangers. I earned enough extra money to enable me to have a holiday in England to assuage my incurable nostalgia.

One night I had a vivid dream. I dreamt I was selling Tupperware. It preyed on my mind all day. I knew the product well, having been to and acted as hostess to the occasional party. One of our Pre-School mothers with whom I was friendly was a dealer of this popular plastic ware — I phoned her.

"Rhonda, can you tell me what is involved in becoming a Tupperware dealer?"

"Come round tomorrow for a cup of tea and I'll explain it to you," she answered.

She told me what was involved and that I would need to hold seven parties to start me off — I knew so many people by this time I had no difficulty in persuading friends to hold a starter party for me. I joined the local distributorship. Rhonda introduced me to her manager Glenys and later to Jenny when Glenys changed to full time employment. We were a happy team.

This was the beginning of five years selling Tupperware part-time and travelling all over the metropolitan area. How glad I was to be a proficient map-reader. Occasionally I was given a "lot number" in an outlying area. These were visible in daylight but often impossible to find in the dark. After a few unnerving experiences I learned to ask the hostess for a landmark to enable me to find her home. I met all kinds of ladies, from a doctor's wife in the hills to a supporting mother in a State house. Not only women, I also had a couple of parties with men who were unfailingly charming and generous.

The actual party I planned with the hostess (or host), encouraging her to invite interested guests and asking if she had any special interests. I also asked if she wanted games. If the answer was an emphatic, "No thank you," I said, "All right, but as everyone likes to take home a small gift I shall play a non-game."

"What do you mean?" she would ask.

"I'll make it simple, such as a random calling of the months, and those with a birthday in that month choose a gift."

"Ah, that's good," she would say, relieved.

Other rather ridiculous games were part of the Tupperware party image and enjoyed by the guests. The little gifts were always useful: a tiny pill container, a strong plastic teaspoon or perhaps a tea bag squeezer. I set up an attractive display of the Tupperware and this well-known product virtually sold itself.

I often reminded myself of the fundamental principles of salesmanship — honesty, courtesy, initiative, punctuality, empathy, appearance, knowledge, fulfilling promises and, above all, discipline and enthusiasm.

After the party I gave everyone a delivery date and reminded the hostess to have the money awaiting me when I delivered the order. All the orders were delivered to me in bulk. My job then was to sort all the goods into the separate hostesses and then package them for each individual. Sadly, when I delivered these bulky items, often travelling up to 40 kms, occasionally the hostess would not have collected the money or some other frustrating mishap had occurred. On the whole, all went smoothly. I made many friends, with the hostesses, the other dealers and my managers. I was a rather low-key saleswoman but in 5½ years sold over $100,000 worth of Tupperware. The profit from this meant I was able to visit England and New Zealand to renew valuable friendships and also visit relatives.

Once more I gained in confidence, as I needed to speak to groups of people. I had the advantage of remembering their names when introduced, a necessary talent I had developed at the beginning of each year with the small children. I also had to organise myself to run a small business. This was the first time in my life that I had handled a cheque book.

I left, to transfer for a short while to selling silk plants and flowers on a similar basis, the big advantage being that I did not make the deliveries. These realistic looking plants and flowers were an innovation then and far superior to graceless plastic flowers.

One evening at about 11p.m. as I was returning home, what I had been dreading happened, a flat tyre; no mobile phones then.

Fortunately I was able to pull off the highway, (luckily this didn't happen on an isolated road) and go into a Fast Food shop to phone the R.A.C. When the poor man arrived we had to lift out masses of plants from the boot to extricate the spare wheel. What a palaver! I decided then and there, that was enough. Goodbye, party plan.

We did not make a lot of profit from it, but dog breeding was a paying hobby — just. We had many valuable delightful litters from our pedigree Shelties. Any money made was always spent on family acquisitions such as our first video recorder, very expensive in those days.

I have a portable massage table and for many years earned a little extra money giving the occasional massage in the client's own home. Again, I met a lot of interesting and congenial people. One lady invariably went to sleep. Another dear, elderly Irish lady, riddled with arthritis, even had it in her scalp.

"What do I have to take off?" she asked anxiously.

"Just what you are comfortable in," I reassured her.

I covered her with towels and soon she felt quite relaxed with me. After a few weeks she discarded her brassière with wild abandon, throwing it on to the chair.

"You should have been a stripper," I teased her.

A lady with no specific aches or pains really needed someone outside the family to confide in. Her husband was unaware that he had been recently diagnosed with Alzheimers disease. She actually pre-deceased him.

I found that receiving a massage seemed to unleash many confidences, but some people enjoyed the relaxation and calming effect of soothing background music. Without exception all the clients were most appreciative and I find it has a two-way benefit, as I enjoy giving a massage as much as much as I enjoy receiving one.

CHAPTER
THIRTY-NINE

Children Growing Up and Grandchildren

Making lemon cordial, the family were keen. Frogs in the lavatory. A letter to the Queen.

When Oliver started Primary school at St Francis Xavier's it was the year they experimented with a new reading system called "Words in Colour". I thought it an excellent method, far better than I.T.A. (Initial Teaching Alphabet) which some schools in England used at the time. There the words were spelt using phonetic symbols as well as the alphabet and had to be eventually unlearned. This technique spelt each word correctly, but each sound was printed in a different colour.

Yellow might be the colour for "oo", so the word zoo, blue, threw, through would be printed yellow. I believe it was to be used for children with reading difficulties. Oliver learned to read quickly and easily, but he was ready and eager and would have succeeded whatever the method.

That year the school's nativity play was dramatised in the playground, the church porch being the setting for the manger. Mary came in, sitting on a real donkey being led by Joseph, but under no circumstances would that animal go near the building. The solemn occasion just caused gales of laughter as Mary dismounted. It made me realise the origin of "as stubborn as a mule".

Both girls completed their primary education at St Francis. I remember one of them returning from school one day saying, "I did neat writing at school today."

The other one said, "I 'did neat' my lunch at school today!"

The year they turned thirteen they transferred to St Joachim's High School, about twenty kilometres from home. In Western Australia this is the usual age to start High School. I was mystified by the V.P.L.C. on Marion's blazer. Originally the convent had been called Victoria Park Ladies College. They wore velour hats in the winter and a white panama hat in the summer, each with a band in school colours.

Aged eight, Oliver passed the exam to go to Trinity College in Perth but we felt he was too immature to cope with the long journey. Instead, aged ten, he started at St Norbert College, about a half an hour on the train. There he remained until he left school aged seventeen.

During their schooldays, each child brought home a report that caused us amusement. One was not remotely interested in Christian Education. The teacher must have racked her brains to think of a remark and

232

decided to write cynically, "— X appreciates Christian qualities in others."

Another who had put on a bit of puberty puppy fat: "— X is an excellent all round student."

The other child came home distraught, having opened and read the report.

"Mrs X says I'm repulsive."

Whatever the teacher may have thought, I hardly thought she would put that in writing. I read the final remarks carefully, relieved to see, "— X is a very *responsive* student."

"I am bored" was an expression never heard in our house. The girls were interested in sewing and crafts, Oliver in electronics, and we were all voracious readers. They had various out of school hobbies. Both girls went to netball practice at the school. Caroline had ballet lessons and both girls enjoyed Ju Jitsu classes for many years. Oliver, not physically aggressive, only went a few times. He enjoyed Cubs but found Boy Scouts a bit too boisterous. Both he and Caroline had singing lessons. I remember his particularly sweet voice aged about seven, singing, "Curraburrawirracanna" the lullaby made popular by Rolf Harris, a West Australian "boy". When quite small we gave Oliver a magnet set with various magnets, steel rods and iron filings. He played with it in bed and must have spilt the iron filings. At the time, he still occasionally wet the bed. I think we were the only people in the neighbourhood hanging out rusted sheets.

For his twelfth birthday his gift was a digital watch. He was thrilled to be the first boy in his class to own one of these innovations. It lasted three weeks before he took it to pieces. Always interested in electronics, his bedroom floor was scattered with bits of old radios and integrated circuits and other technical paraphernalia. He was an individualist, bordering on eccentricity.

Marion and Caroline had always been keen Brownies and Guides. Both achieved the highest award of Queen's Guide. I attended the local celebration and presentations. As usual, Mischa accompanied me. She had learned to proffer her right paw when asked to "shake hands". Guides universally shake hands using their left hand and we had taught her "Guide shake" raising her left paw. The Commissioner was most impressed.

Some weeks later the formal investiture took place at Government House, a most beautiful, grand building in Perth. They were presented to the Governor who is the representative of the Queen. It is rare for sisters to achieve this award together.

Caroline wrote to the Queen to tell her about it and was thrilled a few weeks later when a letter arrived with the Royal Coat of Arms, an acknowledgement on behalf of her Majesty. This insignia on items had fascinated Caroline when she was very small. She noticed it on the jar of Crosse and Blackwell's pickle.

"What is that picture on there for?" she asked.

"It means the Queen eats it," I told her.

Some weeks later I was polishing the shoes and she saw the same insignia on the tin of shoe polish. Her voice tinged with horror, she said innocently, "Does the Queen eat *this*?"

Over the years we had times, like most families, when no one felt co-operative. Sometimes we had an organised afternoon of co-operation, such as "lemon cordial day". Lemons are always plentiful in the winter, so we used the ones from our own over-laden tree. We had a conveyer belt system. One person halved the lemons, the next squeezed them. Initially this was with a hand squeezer, hard work. We invested in a convenient electric one that made it easier and more efficient. Someone else sieved the juice into a jug, added sugar and stirred it. To each pint of juice I then added the magic ingredient, a small amount of sodium metabisulphide, then using a funnel I bottled and labelled it. In three months time it was ready to drink.

The children all did well at High School continuing until their final exams at seventeen, a year younger than their English counterparts. Asked what she wanted to be when she was grown up, Marion aged ten promptly replied, "I'm going to be a Brown Owl." (Brownie leader).

"There's no money in it," I told her.

"I don't care, I'm going to be one."

She was, and revelled in it. (Not like the little girl who was asked what was she going to do when she was as big as Mummy and pertinently replied "diet!")

For a career Marion chose Early Childhood Teaching. After graduating, she taught not far away and spent her first year living at home. In those days, in order to have permanency, one had to teach two years in a country school. She went to Derby (2,391 kilometres north of Perth) in 1980 and never came

235

back. Oh yes, for an occasional visit but that is now her home.

We have always enjoyed any excuse for giving and receiving little gifts but *not* having elaborate parties. On the whole we prefer low key celebrations. I particularly dislike the commercialism of the advertisements that seduce the public to unnecessary extravagance.

Media makes Mum its focus, second Sunday
    soon in May.
What is all this hocus pocus? Don't you know it's
    Mothers' Day?
How much do you love your mother? This is
    what the placards say.
One delight upon another, advertise it's Mothers'
    Day.
How about a fridge or freezer? All the goods are
    on display.
A breadmaker is sure to please her, pamper
    Mum on Mothers' Day.
When I was young, not all this caper, what we
    gave on Mothers' Day
Were little gifts wrapped in paper or flowers in a
    modest spray.

When Marion was twenty-one, she had said she wanted no party, no fuss, just a book of Dirk Bogarde's poems. Oh dear, I searched and searched. I went to theatrical bookshops in London and in desperation wrote to him, care of his publishers. We received a card from the man himself apologising and telling us his

236

only published poems were in the book she had read. We had to re-think her gift.

Her actual birthday coincided with the Brownie meeting. The girls planned a secret surprise party to which I was invited. She must have guessed something was afoot with all the whispering and giggling. At a pre-arranged time they all burst into "Happy Birthday to you". A beautiful cake in the shape of a Brown Owl appeared along with the prettily wrapped gift of a jewellery box. Many of the Brownies gave her little individual presents they had made. Marion really enjoyed that memorable day.

Not being a family who enjoys a lot of extravagant parties, I always jokingly said to the girls, "Either elope or have a joint wedding."

Derby is famous for its bottle-shaped boab trees and each year in winter has a Boab Festival. In 1983 Marion, as well as teaching, ran the Brownie pack there. She phoned me, "Guess what Mum, the Brownies came second in the Boab parade . . . oh . . . and I got married this afternoon."

When I recovered from the shock, I retaliated with "Oh yes, and who to?" knowing full well that she had been seeing Carl for a while.

Caroline joined Oliver at St Norbert College after they became co-educational, for her final two years. She did well in her Tertiary Admittance Examination and chose the more practical career of the Child Care Course. This qualified her to care for children from birth to age six.

The course was based originally on the qualifications I had attained many years previously in England, the N.N.E.B. (National Nursery Examination Board.)

Later Carrie found, as I did, that it was an excellent preparation for motherhood. Soon after she qualified, she married a handsome policeman. It was a quiet wedding performed by a marriage celebrant and with just Craig's immediate family and ours, which of course included Eve and Mac. We hoped they would live happily ever after. Sadly, after some years they separated and divorced. How fortunate that she had a qualification that enabled her to work school hours at a local Catholic Pre-primary. She has been a devoted mother to her three children and coped admirably on her own.

I only gave two pieces of advice to my children. One, get your priorities right; the other, remember your priorities change. I often have to remind myself severely to live up to these maxims.

Oliver played a guitar and sang in a small local band. Scientific subjects had a great fascination for him. He too did very well in his T.A.E. exams but decided against a University career. He moved out of home when only nineteen, but moved back again later, as so often happens with families. Each of my children was a year younger to leave home than the previous one. Marion was twenty-one when she transferred to Derby, Carrie twenty when she married.

As a child, Oliver tended to be a loner, by choice. The teachers were quite concerned.

"Mrs Day," they informed me, "Oliver is not a good mixer."

Sound systems were his speciality. He "mixed" for many bands and was in constant demand. I could not help smiling to myself remembering the teacher's remark. After a few years his reputation was such that he received a phone call.

"Oliver Day?"

"Yes, that's me."

"We need you in Melbourne urgently to help install the sound systems in the new World Congress Centre, can you fly here tomorrow?"

"Of course," Oliver agreed, getting a few more details.

He enjoyed the cosmopolitan atmosphere and very different lifestyle. One evening that winter he phoned me.

"Mum, I was driving in the hills and I thought a truck had spilt a load of polystyrene beads by the road."

It was the first time he could remember seeing snow. His career blossomed in the Eastern States. We saw him rarely.

In 1984 Carrie (as she insisted on being called once she left school) and Craig produced our first grandchild, Katie. Marion and Carl's Rachel arrived six weeks later. I had hardly absorbed the delight of grannyhood when my pleasure was doubled. Within four years I was the proud possessor of seven beautiful grandchildren. A bit of a shock to the system! Carrie has two daughters and a son and Marion a daughter and three sons, whom I see very rarely because of the vast distance. Although

Derby, like Armadale, is in Western Australia, it is a similar distance from us as London is from Moscow.

On the occasions she has visited us, Marion is usually accompanied by two children while the other two stay with Carl to take care of the property. Their requests are very few and usually simple. When they were small, traffic lights were a great fascination. At the mature ages of fourteen and fifteen they asked, "Granny, please can we go to Carousel shopping centre?"

"Of course," I answered, taking them there the following day, with Marion too. "Now where would you like to go?"

They gave me the name of the large department store. The attraction? Escalators! They spent a happy time on them while we shopped. Their other unsophisticated wish was to be driven to the top of our hill at night, so they could admire the thousands of twinkling lights over the city. Derby is so flat they need an artificial ramp for learners to master a hill start when taking their driving lessons.

I visited Marion when her two youngest were about three and four and could not remember me. They stared at me open mouthed.

"What's the matter with me, Marion?"

"Don't worry, Mum, they've never seen a granny before."

A large proportion of the population are full blood aborigines and most of the white population are there on a short term contract.

240

They had a very unsophisticated lifestyle on a few hectares of land. Initially their shower was some distance from the house and they kept a Childrens python there to keep the frogs down! No, it was not a pet. It was named after a Dr Childrens — true!

By the time I visited them, they had a bathroom — of sorts. No shower at the time, Marion bathed standing in a bowl tipping water over herself.

"Be careful, Mum," she advised me. "Don't you try and sit in it, you might get stuck."

The children squatted around me watching, slightly disconcerting. Marion reassured me, "They just want to see what a granny looks like without any clothes."

"The same as a mummy," I told them, "only there is more of her."

Frogs were everywhere. The stainless steel walls were wallpapered with frogs at dusk — Ugh! To my horror a large one looked up at me from the inside of the lavatory bowl. I returned to Perth very constipated.

Her kitchen had a roof but no walls. The stainless steel sink used a hose instead of a tap and the water drained into a bucket. They lived well. Carl fished and exchanged fresh barramundi for a "beast" from a local station and they grew their own vegetables. Their large freezer was always well stocked.

Carl's health had deteriorated and he was no longer able to be employed by the Agricultural Protection Board. He looked after the little ones very competently when Marion returned to teaching. "Miss Marion," as she has always been known, has taught the second generation of children and really loves her chosen career.

Grandchildren are very forthright. One asked me, "Why doesn't your skin fit you any more, Granny?" and "Were you born with those stripes on your face?"

Another one, aged about three, asked me, "Do cockroaches eat little boys?"

"No," I assured him, "just dirty things."

A wicked glint in his eye, he asked, "Well then, do they eat grannies?"

One day I was showing a simple picture book to one of the little girls when she was learning to talk.

"What is that?" I asked, pointing to a teddy bear.

"Bear," she replied.

"And that?" pointing to a picture of a hairbrush.

"Brush," she said.

"And what do we do with it?" She pretended to brush her hair.

"Clever girl, and what are those?" I pointed to some red shoes on the page.

"Shoo-shoes," she proudly told me.

"And where do they go?" I prompted. Very well trained she said, "Away."

Once I was invited to watch their Catholic Pre-school Nativity play, charmed to see the little five year olds performing. Afterwards Father Christmas and his sack arrived to be greeted by twenty excited children.

"First of all, who can tell me what is special about Christmas?"

A lot of little hands shot up.

242

"I know, I know, Santa Claus brings us toys."

"Yes," he agreed "But I'm thinking of something else. I'll give you a clue. It is someone special's birthday on Christmas Day."

Again a forest of raised hands.

"All right, you tell me," he pointed to a small, eager faced boy.

"Christmas Day is my Auntie Betty's birthday," he told us.

Children are so ingenuous, their innocent remarks have delighted me over the years, from my own children, my pre-school children and then my grandchildren.

CHAPTER
FORTY

Pot-Pourri

Giving and receiving gifts gave me lots of pleasure. I loved collecting bargains at the local "Trash and Treasure".

"Off we go with a rumble-oh and an um diddle eye-doh pling." We always recited this daft phrase when we were going out with the children. I've no idea where or how it originated but like many family sayings it became part of our lives, like "wakling" the dog. Very many years ago we saw a misprint in a newspaper. "Woman attacked whilst wakling her dog". From that day our dogs have always been "wakled". I remember the Budgies Stuart coming home from school saying he'd got a "furly". Cousin Eve was most confused until she realised he had "got off early". I'm one who gets a "pearly". Yes I get up early! We have lots of silly expressions like many families do.

One tradition we have is "the Christmas tree". Like most people we have a decorated tree complete with Susie our fairy doll on the top. In the morning we exchange our gifts, but we always keep a bit of excitement for after our traditional Christmas lunch.

We put a gift on the tree for each other to a rigid or challenging stipulation. I might suggest, "This year whatever we buy must fit into a matchbox" or "This year the cost must not be more than two dollars" or "This year we must all find something that is red."

Each person had to use their ingenuity to buy or make four gifts. The twenty little parcels looked very decorative.

As soon as lunch finished, the clamour started.

"Can we have the Christmas tree presents *now*?"

Soon we were all unwrapping our little gifts. It prolonged the excitement of the day.

BOOZIE SUSIE

The story of this saga starts in 1958
We'd bought a perfect Christmas tree, tall and
    green and straight.
We had tinsel and baubles but nothing for the
    top
So I took my shopping basket and went off to
    the shop.
We had to walk in those days, we didn't have a
    car,
I looked at decorations and nearly bought a star.
But a tiny little voice went buzzing through my
    head
"Don't get a star, a fairy doll is what you need
    instead."
Alas, our lack of finance meant that they were far
    too dear,

245

Off I went to Woolworths that very fateful year,
There I saw a plastic doll that really closed her
eyes,
Her hair was blonde, her eyes were blue, she was
the perfect size.
I bought her and I took her home. I found some
scraps of lace
And made her clothes, a tiny wand, then fixed
her in her place.
There she reigned each Christmas, queen of all
that she surveyed.
She saw each baby growing up and watched
them as they played.
At Christmastide she sat aloft, our loyal overseer,
We name our fairy Susie and cherished her each
year.
Decorations came and went but Susie was
intrepid,
But as the years went rolling by she really looked
decrepit.
Her clothes were old, her wand was bent, her
crown was all askew
So we gave her a refurbishing, she looked as
good as new.
But those eyelids drooped, her hair looked sad,
her face distinctly woozy,
We gave the nickname and it stuck, and called
her "Boozy Susie".
Debauched she sat atop the tree, pie-eyed but
still ornate.
A special birthday she enjoyed in 1998.

We put the record player on, a celebration
  planned,
And fixed a tiny plastic glass into her willing
  hand.
You may think it unkind of us, I know it's rather
  naughty,
We sang the song "Nobody loves a fairy now
  she's forty".
She didn't seem offended, so a photograph I
  took,
To keep it for posterity and treasure in my book.

There were no cinemas nearer than Perth so we only went there on school holidays. Locally we had a drive-in cinema. We paid at the entry booth. The ground was laid in waves and one parked carefully, tilting upwards to focus on the huge screen. We unhooked the speaker from the adjacent post and hooked it on to the car window. These nights were a real excitement for us uninitiated "poms". The stars were so bright in the clear sky one felt as if one could reach up and pluck one. Obviously we only went to the drive-in when it was fine. Children, often dressed in their night clothes, would run to the onsite shop in the interval for lollies (sweets) or ice-creams. It was a common sight to see people in their dressing gowns watering their gardens. It took us a while to adjust to the informality of Australian life.

In England I always enjoyed going to the January sales. I love bargains and attend local garage sales in the perpetual hope of finding a "treasure" whether or not it is of value. Every Sunday morning for many years has seen me driving to the "Trash and Treasure" (car boot sale) about ten miles away. Toys and plants predominate. Many of the stall holders are regular dealers, rarely a bargain there. Often when someone is moving house, they might have a garage sale initially, then bring their bits and pieces to sell really cheaply. I have bought some wonderful things over the years, and lots of rubbish! Our dear friend Leo, a talented engraver, made me some earrings and brooches saying "I love bargains" and "I love garage sales". They cause great amusement.

Once I bought a floor polisher still in its box. When I removed it at home, I found amongst the bits of fluff in the bottom of the box, an old curtain ring.

"Come and have a look at this, Don," I called. "It looks like a wedding ring."

I could tell by its weight that it must be gold. The following week I informed the Rotarians who ran the Trash and Treasure about the inscribed ring and left my phone number. No one ever claimed it, I have it still.

I have bought some much needed extra bookcases very reasonably. Folk often ask me to look for items such as a lid for an obsolete design casserole, or a specific book. It is quite amazing but sooner or later I manage to find them. I usually find something I want, but of late I have tried to use a bit of discipline and say, "I want it but do I *need* it?"

Yes, it is a compulsion and I *do* buy some things that don't work and go straight into the dustbin. Ask me about what I really collect and the answer is everything.

I have a comprehensive collection of ornamental ginger jars, some very lovely ones amongst them. Another collection is a bit unusual, kaleidoscopes. As a child they always fascinated me and I still delight in the variety of patterns they produce. I have one with shapes that move, a musical clockwork one, another is exquisitely handmade locally of stained glass. A tiny wooden egg on a brass stand holds another and I have many, many more.

I collect limerick books of all sorts and love this definition by "anonymous".

> The limerick packs laughs anatomical
> Into space that is quite economical.
> Those that I've seen
> So seldom are clean
> And the clean ones so seldom are comical.

And this one about Eve —

> My friend knew a typist called Eve
> Said, "Your boss is too good to believe,
> You can't type, you can't spell
> Why's he pay you so well?"
> Eve answered "I cannot conceive."

My personal lavatory has a tiny bookcase where I keep most of my humorous books. Originally it was just for my collection of lavatory books. I have quite a few on the history of the lavatory and many more on lavatory humour.

Don tried to control our large sloping garden. He grew many plants in his shade house. In England we had a glass greenhouse to attract the sun, in Australia a similar construction but covered in shade cloth to protect the plants from the sun. He had a thriving vegetable garden and many roses, fruit trees and flowers. We also had a strawberry bed. I went to pick some one day and went rushing into the house.

"Don, Don, come quickly, there's an awful, dangerous 'something' in there."

Don followed me rather tentatively carrying the hoe in case it was a snake. Most snakes in Australia, except pythons, are poisonous. He poked the hoe into the bed and saw a gaping, blue mouth.

"Ugh, that's it."

I backed away shuddering. Don laughed.

"Don't be silly, it's only a "sleepy", he reassured me. These are the bob-tail lizards that we often saw squashed on the road.

They amble along slowly and sleepily, hence their nickname. These scaly, fat reptiles are not poisonous but if provoked can give a painful bite. They love strawberries.

Sometimes by the roadside one would see a dead kangaroo that had been hit by a vehicle. They sleep most of the day but at twilight bound along with absolutely no road sense. Recently I heard why one never sees a dead crow by the road. They are in pairs and one acts as a look out. When he sees a vehicle coming he calls "Car, car!"

Some years ago my friend Muriel and I spent a few days in Melbourne to see "Phantom of the Opera". I took the opportunity to spend some quality time with Oliver who was living there. We went to Fitzroy

Gardens at dusk to see the possums. A small crowd had gathered, I hadn't realised it was to watch him. As a very young child, animals were always attracted to him, I have a grandchild with a similar affinity. These possums allowed him to hand feed them, to the appreciation of the bystanders. He had always liked animals but never considered a career with them. Electronics and music were his priorities, not necessarily in that order.

Carrie wrote to the Queen. I too have sent letters to assorted people I admire and have treasured their replies. I have the letter from the author Faith Addis, the card from Dirk Bogarde and the note from Penelope Keith. I wrote to the author Simon Brett as I loved his "Mrs Pargeter" books and I received a charming reply. I have letters from the talented baritone Ian Wallace, the comedian Jimmy Edwards and a signed photo for the family from that other clever humorist Ronnie Barker: another collection of mine, a few autographs.

I have always been eager to learn, as I often feel so ignorant when in stimulating company. Some years before retirement, I joined Trinity School for Seniors, which is held on two days a week in Perth. I went to classes each Thursday and learned conversational French, listened to lectures on a variety of subjects and also joined the dancing class. This was a totally new venture for me and great fun. We learned folk dances from various countries and at the end of the year danced on the stage at Perth Town Hall. The French class also performed an amusing item. The audience

251

consisted of other members of the school. Altogether a stimulating and enjoyable day each week.

Twenty-two has been a significant number in our family. Don's birthday is 22.11.22. We arrived in Australia January 22 and we stayed in the house we built here for twenty-two years. This was by far the longest I had ever lived anywhere. The family had left and, although the position was convenient, the big steep garden was a constant battle. The thirty kilometres from here to the coast was flat and we had wonderful views. We faced due west. Oliver and I, being real romantics, for years had gazed at the magnificent, brilliant sunsets. The Darling Scarp starts in Armadale and Don wanted to stay in the hills, *but* he wanted a flat garden. There were only very few vacant blocks and all were steep. I looked at a number of older houses for sale but found nothing suitable. Don and my opinions do not always coincide. We knew we wanted to remain in Armadale, then I found this house. We both liked it. It was about sixteen years old, very well built to an original design. The owners were returning to England to be with their daughter. The paved garden was almost flat. A couple of years before I retired we had the big upheaval of moving house, but never regretted it.

I had made up my mind to retire on my birthday but earlier that year had been quite ill and hospitalised briefly. I struggled on, as I do not easily give up. Les the headmaster very kindly said, "Are you sure you are well enough to continue until the end of third term? After all these years here, I'd like to see you go with a bang, not a whimper."

His wishes were granted. I had a wonderful party at the Pre-school. The children came in fancy dress and I was presented with many gifts from the school and the teachers. I also received individual presents from the children. I gave the Pre-primary school a native frangipani tree which I ceremoniously planted. I see that it is thriving. The Committee had a special plaque made. At the school assembly that week I had a presentation and altogether was made to feel very special. Les and Dorothy had gone to such a lot of trouble, but it was certainly appreciated.

The most satisfying elements of my life have all involved nurturing and caring, hence my love of children and pets. I consider myself fortunate not only to have been blessed with children, but also having the opportunity of working with them.

My feelings about retirement were ambivalent. I loved my work, but I also felt ready to leave. I now use F words as my philosophy in life. As long as I have my

Fitness
Faculties
Freedom and
Finance

Then I'll have . . . *fun*

Speech for Mrs Day.

Mrs Day,

Many students from Kelmscott primary school remember the outstanding job you did teaching us at Pre-Primary. You led us to the excellent standards of this school and prepared us greatly for year one. This special chair assembly is a great opportunity to thank-you and wish you a happy future. I'm sure that everyone would like you to visit and keep in touch. You are a real contrubitor to the Pre-Primary and school. On behalf of the school Josie would like to present you with these flowers.

Thank-you Mrs Day.

ISIS publish a wide range of books in large print, from fiction to biography. Any suggestions for books you would like to see in large print or audio are always welcome. Please send to the Editorial department at:

ISIS Publishing Ltd.
7 Centremead
Osney Mead
Oxford OX2 0ES
(01865) 250 333

A full list of titles is available free of charge from:
Ulverscroft large print books

(UK)
The Green
Bradgate Road, Anstey
Leicester LE7 7FU
Tel: (0116) 236 4325

(Australia)
P.O Box 953
Crows Nest
NSW 1585
Tel: (02) 9436 2622

(USA)
1881 Ridge Road
P.O Box 1230, West Seneca,
N.Y. 14224-1230
Tel: (716) 674 4270

(Canada)
P.O Box 80038
Burlington
Ontario L7L 6B1
Tel: (905) 637 8734

(New Zealand)
P.O Box 456
Feilding
Tel: (06) 323 6828

Details of **ISIS** complete and unabridged audio books are also available from these offices. Alternatively, contact your local library for details of their collection of **ISIS** large print and unabridged audio books.